Jesus
on
Parenting

Jesus
on
Parenting

Teresa Whitehurst

BakerBooks
Grand Rapids, Michigan

Published by Baker Books
a division of Baker Publishing Group
P.O. Box 6287, Grand Rapids, MI 49516-6287
www.bakerbooks.com

Paperback edition published 2004
ISBN 0-8010-6529-1

Previously published under the title *How Would Jesus Raise a Child?*

Printed in the United States of America

The Library of Congress has cataloged the hardcover editon as follows:
Whitehurst, Teresa, 1954-
    How would Jesus raise a child? / Teresa Whitehurst.
        p.   cm.
    Includes bibliographical references.
    ISBN 0-8010-1250-3
    1. Parenting—Religious aspects—Christianity. 2. Jesus Christ—Teachings.
    I. Title.
BV4529 .W55 2003
248.8 '45—dc21   2002152039

To my loving, spiritually grounded family, Tom and Ouida Whitehurst, Sascha and Peter Demerjian, Isadora Pennington, and David and Bonnie Whitehurst, and to my supportive friends and colleagues

To the African American women who taught me about life and the need for faith as they took care of me when I was young (I can almost hear those gospel spirituals on the radio), especially Eddie Mae

And to Lisa Steinberg, whose young life was cut short by those who could not see, parent, or treasure you as Jesus would. I kept my promise—this is for you, and for all parents and children, from God, through me

Contents

Acknowledgments

I used to wonder why authors acknowledged so many people for helping them make the dream of their book become a reality. Now I know. Once a thing is done, we realize that we didn't do it on our own. For their commitment and expertise in the publication process, I'd like to thank Dean Schoenwald, my editor Vicki Crumpton, copyeditors Mary Suggs and Wendy Wetzel, the design and marketing teams, and the whole Baker team. My desire to use what I've learned for the sake of others was inspired by numerous teachers and professors, especially Dr. Valerian Derlega at Old Dominion University and Dr. Paul Dokecki and Dr. Robert Newbrough at Vanderbilt University. From my mentors, including many authors referenced in this book whom I've never met in person but have come to know through their works, I realized that, contrary to popular opinion, one can indeed combine reason, scholarship, and faith.

I am very grateful to my colleagues at Harvard University, particularly Dr. David Perkins and his concept of "symbolic conduct." Symbolic conduct succinctly describes the vitally important guidance that we can "read" in Jesus' behavior, thus learning more from him than through words alone. Additionally, my understanding of parents as leaders has been enriched from his analysis of the kinds of leadership that are characteristic of "intelligent organizations" (and families are small organizations), in which people feel free to take reasonable risks, innovate, and trust and support one another.

Leonard Maluf, S.S.L., S.T.D., professor of philosophy and New Testament at Blessed John XXIII National Seminary in Weston, Massachusetts, answered my endless questions with patience and care. I benefited greatly from his vast knowledge of the Gospels, as well as his mentoring and encouragement throughout the research and writing process. His high standards of academic excellence in theology and exegesis motivated me to always look deeper, gleaning every nugget of wisdom from the Scriptures without relying on pat answers or common assumptions.

I so wish that I could thank Mother Teresa for all that her example has taught me, but that time has passed. Perhaps, however, I can say thank you to her spirit, which lives on in many, many people who care for the very young, the very old, the sick, and all those who are suffering spiritually. These men and women are—often with low wages or none at all—living out her divinely inspired vision. At the 331st commencement of Harvard University, she said:

> And you will, I'm sure, ask me: Where is that hunger in our country? Where is that nakedness in our country? Where is that homelessness in our country? Yes, there *is* hunger. Maybe not the hunger for a piece of bread. But there is a terrible hunger for love. We all experience that in our lives—the pain, the loneliness. We must have the courage to recognize that the poor you may have *right in your own family*. Find them, love them, put your love for them in a loving action. For in loving them, *you are loving God himself.* God bless you.

Introduction

Jesus never married and never had children, yet in one sense he did raise children, scores and scores of them. First he took on a motley crew of unschooled, impulsive, and often undisciplined fishermen and other working people and somehow instilled in them a new morality, a new spirit, as well as a guiding vision, self-control, and self-confidence. Later he trained others in small groups and large crowds, in one-on-one conversations and in casual exchanges during his journeys. Whether you're a Christian or come from another faith, you may admire Jesus for his character, his revolutionary teachings, his gentleness, his courage, or all of the above. If you don't stop there but sincerely commit yourself to learning what he taught and how he taught it, slowly but surely his words will begin to echo in your mind. One day, without knowing how, you'll realize that you have indeed begun to raise your child as Jesus would.

The idea of parenting your child as Jesus would is compelling, inspiring. Perhaps you've wanted to do this in the past, looking for a book on parenting that refers exclusively to the teachings and actions of Jesus. Certainly, scores of books, some of them outstanding, have been written according to scriptural teaching, but what they have in common is the most unfortunate omission of one parental model in particular—Jesus. Sometimes an author gives a nod to the New Testament, but such references are few, usually to the Gospel and Epistle writ-

11

ers who wrote about family life, rather than to Jesus himself. You may not realize what's amiss but you probably sense that something in those books, despite their good ideas, is missing. Like a piano chord played with one wrong note, there is something discordant about parenting books, supposedly representing Christianity, that are based on Scripture but not on Jesus' parenting model.

The omission of reference to Jesus is not limited, however, to parenting books. It may come as a surprise to many readers that even the education of priests and ministers may lack significant study of Jesus' words and actions. Joseph Girzone, author of the Joshua series, writes:

> When I began touring the country, talking about Jesus' life and teaching, I was shocked at the response of people who kept telling me they never heard talks about Jesus' life before. One very holy priest . . . expressed surprise that I could talk about Jesus for an hour and a half. When I asked him why he was so shocked, he reminded me that we had never been taught about Jesus in the seminary. We were taught theology and scripture and canon law, and so many other courses, but no one ever taught any courses about Jesus Himself as a person. . . . I got the same response from Protestants. One seminarian for the priesthood told me she had applied to five prestigious seminaries. . . . She asked the admissions officers at each one if their seminary taught courses about Jesus. She was shocked when the answer each time was "No, but we teach courses on Christology as electives."[1]

I wrote this book because over the years, without quite realizing it, I was writing it in my mind. In every worship service and at home with my Bible, I read Jesus' words over and over again, imagining how he must have looked and sounded as he spoke or acted in each situation. This practice allowed me to vividly see and hear him as I read the Gospels. As a parent, I found that whenever I felt discouraged, irritated, hurt, worried, or overwhelmed, I could go "watch the movie" in my mind, imagining what Jesus would do in whatever situation I was facing. Even when I was so confused and upset that I couldn't think clearly, Jesus' principles miraculously resurfaced when I paused to let my heart and mind prayerfully relax, watching and hearing him respond to my child . . . and to me.

Having been raised in a very religious environment, I naturally picked up a zest for spiritual knowledge and experience and learned about Jesus at an early age. Over the years I attended many churches, savoring each congregation's unique way of worshiping and coming together as a community. I loved hearing the different forms of music and teaching and learned that each denomination has its own special gifts, not duplicated elsewhere.

In many houses of worship, however, I saw parents locked into frequent destructive struggles with their children while trying to raise them according to selected verses from the Scriptures—but not according to Jesus' words and actions. Unfortunately, the verses they'd been told to use to guide their parenting supported a power-focused or indifferent stance toward babies and children. I witnessed the stress this caused to both parent and child and the damage to the connection between them. The "good" children were those who became passive and outwardly obedient. They seemed to be doing fine while they were young, but as I watched them over the years, I saw them turn into the kind of judgmental, legalistic religious people Jesus repeatedly warned his followers not to become. Some of these children moved away from religion altogether as they got older. Some returned later in life, but some did not.

This reliance on everything-but-Jesus for parenting advice seemed too great a risk to take. Many people say, "Well, that's the way my parents raised me, and I turned out fine." Perhaps (though one wonders if their spiritual lives are as "fine" as their external appearance), but I wouldn't want to take that chance.

Who can tell which child can endure parenting-as-usual or being raised according to methods that Jesus would not condone? I decided that my children would be raised as Jesus would raise them—as closely, that is, as an imperfect parent like me could follow his teachings and example.

As a psychologist working with children and families, I noticed that parents who followed the principles that Jesus taught (whether or not they realized they were doing so) tended to have strong parent-child relationships and optimistic attitudes toward handling problems as they arose, while parents using either parenting-as-usual or legalistic religious parenting methods complained of recurring conflicts and frayed connections between family members.

Decades of study, not only of the Scriptures but of commentaries, scholarly works, and popular books on the subject as well, have enabled me to assemble Jesus' teachings and behaviors for you in this book as they apply to our sacred role as parents. It is my hope that you will examine them closely as you read, so that whenever a new problem or need arises, you will hear Jesus speak and see him in action quite vividly in your mind and heart. For this is how you will begin to raise your child as Jesus would.

Looking beyond the Obvious

Jesus did not give direct advice on specific parenting problems, and even if he had, two thousand years ago he couldn't have taught us how to handle cell-phone use, dating, violent video games, or the Internet. Most if not all popular Christian parenting writers have limited themselves to direct Scripture references to child rearing—which means that Jesus' own teaching will necessarily be rarely mentioned or omitted altogether. This seems to be the primary rationale for not basing parenting advice on Jesus' teaching and example. Yet this has not been an obstacle for other areas of interest, such as business ethics, personal development, and community life. It seems that in nearly all areas except parenting, many books have been written to guide the individual toward a mode of interaction and communication with others—an interpersonal ethic, if you will—that is based on Jesus and his message (for example, *Jesus, CEO* by Laurie Beth Jones and *Spiritual Fitness* by Doris Donnelly).

In the Old Testament there are many great lessons to be learned from dramatic stories of suffering, victory, happiness, and defeat. The Old Testament contains the Ten Commandments, which are what we might term the "minimum daily requirement" for religious persons. And it contains several specific instructions congruent with Judaic law and custom prior to and during Jesus' time. Some of these are wise and beautiful, but some Old Testament advice, such as the advice to use a rod to beat children, has been hotly debated for centuries, and a few verses are so frightful that they are carefully ignored by Jews and Christians alike. Just one example is the parenting advice given in Deuteronomy 21:20–21 for handling rebellious teens: Stone them to death.

The Paradox

Many theologians have recognized in Jesus' words and actions the best model for our own words and actions. Long ago Thomas à Kempis (1380–1471) wrote the masterpiece that has been studied by Christians across denominations, *The Imitation of Christ*—the first systematic delineation of Jesus' words and actions for the purpose of modeling oneself after him. Countless thinkers have observed in Jesus a remarkable and challenging role model for relationships with others, self, and God. You too may have sensed in Jesus a model and guide for your life. Yet all too often we're told that such a goal is impossible and should be abandoned. What are the arguments of these naysayers? They include the following common statements:

1. Jesus was God. It's unrealistic and impractical to try to be like God.
2. Jesus was born in a manger and died on the cross to save humanity. Everything between those two events is interesting but not essential.
3. To be saved from sin, all that is needed is belief in Jesus as the Son of God. There's no need to actually do anything differently here on earth.
4. Those "bad people" out there, not believers, need to learn from Jesus.

Paradoxically, this idea—that Jesus is perfect, so we needn't worry about actually trying to faithfully follow those difficult things he taught—can make Christians less likely than people of other faiths to live according to his precepts. M. K. Gandhi demonstrates the seriousness with which seekers from other religious traditions take Jesus' actual teachings and lifestyle:

> What does Jesus mean to me? To me, he was one of the greatest teachers humanity has ever had. To his believers, he was God's only begotten son. Could the fact that I do or do not accept this belief make Jesus have any more or less influence on my life? Is all the grandeur of his teaching and his doctrine to be forbidden to me? I cannot believe so.[2]

> Christian: one who believes that the New Testament is a divinely inspired book admirably suited to the spiritual needs of his neighbor.
>
> Ambrose Bierce

Gandhi, coming from his own religious tradition, did not believe in Jesus' divinity; therefore he didn't dismiss Jesus' teachings or example as "too perfect" for him to take seriously and incorporate into his life.

16

Conventional wisdom and the way our parents did things are helpful but not sufficient. Being human, parents tend to resort to the same methods they've witnessed other parents using, their own especially. When their child doesn't respond well, they repeat what they've already tried, only this time louder, harder, or with greater gusto. Such tactics create temporary change at best, and the seeds of longer-term problems are often planted in the process. The child has not been transformed from the inside out, because the parent hasn't been. It's difficult to change a paradigm—the way we view the world or some part of it—especially when it has to do with something we care deeply about. That's why even scientists can't let go of a familiar paradigm until they've encountered many, many failed attempts to make new problems fit into the old model and respond to old methods. When Jesus told the story about putting new wine into old wineskins, he was getting at this very point. Trying to integrate his new paradigm into our old ways of thinking, feeling, and behaving will remove the value of his gift to humanity.

Jesus didn't ask people to follow him without giving them a map. Before sending his disciples out to preach the Good News to others, he made sure they understood the basic principles underlying his many teachings and good works. He didn't burden them with a laundry list of dos and don'ts; rather, he trusted their ability to think for themselves and to deal with any problem or difficult situation by applying the principles he had taught them.

In similar fashion, this book assumes that its readers are intelligent human beings who can learn the principles that Jesus taught and begin to think through their daily parenting challenges and long-term dreams for their children as he would. No book could ever cover every specific problem or need that parents will encounter, such as the three-year-old boy who kept putting marbles in his nose (true story!) or the teenage girl who, months after her mother died, began wearing a small wooden skeleton around her neck and dressing daily in black. Silly or serious, the problems parents face are too many and varied to address specifically, point by point, in any book. What we can do, however, is learn the ways in which Jesus would size up situations, see into a child's heart to diagnose the true problem, and guide the parent toward responding in a way that would strengthen the child's connection to both the parent and God.

The House Built on the Rock

Wouldn't it feel great to know that whether you live in a shack or a mansion, you are building for your children a spiritual home, set on a firm foundation that will withstand every wind, every thunderstorm, every jolt they'll encounter throughout their lives? This was what Jesus promised his followers if they heard and put into practice his teachings. They would receive a remarkable inner stability and strength amid all the joys and sorrows, adventures and dangers, successes and disappointments of life.

> "Why do you call me, 'Lord, Lord,' and do not do what I say? I will show you what he is like who comes to me and hears my words and puts them into practice. He is like a man building a house, who dug down deep and laid the foundation on rock. When a flood came, the torrent struck that house but could not shake it, because it was well built. But the one who hears my words and does not put them into practice is like a man who built a house on the ground without a foundation. The moment the torrent struck that house, it collapsed and its destruction was complete."
>
> Luke 6:46–48 NIV

This "foundation on rock" remains the inheritance of all who strive to live according to Jesus' charter, the sum of all his teachings. Jesus made it clear that no ethnic, economic, cultural, or national differences were relevant spiritually. He was offering to all the people of the world a new interpersonal ethic, a higher level of morality, and an altogether different relationship with God. Whether you're reading this in Ireland, Africa, Japan, Korea, India, Italy, Lebanon, or the United States, you're invited to take God up on this promise that Jesus so boldly made, for your sake, for your family's sake, and for all who will be touched by you and yours.

To achieve this firm foundation, you need to begin to get a picture in your mind of how things could be. Even if your relationship with your child is already quite good, there are ways in which it could be even better. And if you are worried about your child, concerned that he or she may be troubled, has become alienated or distant, or seems to need something you can't quite put your finger on, you are picking up important signals through your "parenting antennae" that should not be ignored. Consider just a few of the differences between the worldly approach and Jesus' approach in terms of perceiving problems, setting goals, and helping a person mature and develop his or her potential:

How would most people raise a child?	How would Jesus raise a child?
Their time frame **Short-term:** They aim at immediate change and assume it has failed if they don't see quick results.	*His time frame* **Long-term:** He would aim for lasting change, which usually evolves over time.
Their focus regarding behavior **Observable outcome:** They reward or punish according to obvious, external results.	*His focus regarding behavior* **Process of change:** He would encourage every effort along the way, even tiny internal changes.
Their priority **Society's demands:** They value fitting in with others above all else; conformity with other people or tradition.	*His priority* **God's desires:** He would value attunement with God above all else, following his teachings.
Their perceptual and thinking style **Black and white:** They judge situations or persons as all good or all bad, all right or all wrong.	*His perceptual and thinking style* **Colorful:** He would examine all sides of a situation or person to understand deeply and make wise decisions.
Their stance in conversations **Certainty:** They assume they already know others' (and child's) feelings, concerns, reasoning, and needs.	*His stance in conversations* **Curiosity:** He would want to know how people think and how they have come to feel and behave as they do; he would ask.

How would your child—and you—feel and behave differently if your inner lives were built on the sturdy foundation promised by Jesus? How might your child change in mind, heart, and behavior if you began today to learn how Jesus would raise a child and put that knowledge into practice? What transformations might occur in you?

Focusing on the Internal

The contrasts in the table above can be distilled into one overarching distinction—the external versus the internal. Jesus always emphasized the internal self, for that is where the kingdom of God is sown or not sown, nurtured or starved. Never satisfied with external appearances, he repeatedly honed in on the spirit behind a person's words, actions, or attitudes. These contrasts, which Jesus illustrated in many stories and conversations, should be kept in mind as you read this book and reflect on your own experiences years ago as a child and now as a parent. So much becomes clear to us when we sit quietly, pausing to think about what we're reading in terms of our own lives. It's important to give yourself time, lots of time, as you process what Jesus taught with his words and through his very deliberate actions.

"Let all who have ears, hear," Jesus said again and again. The choice is indeed ours, but we are not left with merely a nice idea or vision. Jesus provides for us a model for parenting, a remarkably detailed blueprint for guiding those in our care that will, if we are faithful to it, keep both our children and ourselves on the right path.

The Blueprint

Jesus walked the earth as a revolutionary hero of a very different sort than we usually see. His teachings, delivered with gentle confidence, bothered the rich and powerful of his day. His refusal to back down from his convictions threatened those in authority, especially those who were accustomed to enforcing religious rules, deciding who did and didn't measure up. Yet the poor and the weak, the young and the old, the oppressed and those who yearned for freedom, justice, and mercy, these people flocked around him. He comforted the suffering, encouraged the timid, rejuvenated the despairing, and boldly rewrote the social contract. He rejected the world's way of measuring a person's righteousness, teaching God's way instead.

Teaching with Words

Jesus carefully observed the person with whom he was speaking and tailored his words to make sure he or she would understand. With fishermen he spoke of fishing; with farmers he spoke of farming; with Pharisees he spoke of law and Scripture; with workers he spoke of wages and work agreements; with women drawing water from wells he spoke of streams of living water. He did not speak in difficult, theoretical terms, expecting his listeners to understand. Clearly Jesus was sensitive to the capabilities and experiences of those with whom he was speaking.

Jesus differed from other teachers too by teaching an altogether new way of viewing everything in life, including one's motives, others' behaviors, and life itself. Jesus told stories that inspired people to reflect and question their assumptions and their society's values. He let ideas sink in slowly or rise up from within. He didn't want people to passively consume his words but to think deeply about them.

Teaching through Behavior

Jesus knew that people were watching him, and he was ever mindful that

> The great thing in this world is not so much where we stand, as in what direction we are moving.
>
> Oliver Wendell Holmes

21

actions speak louder than words. By closely observing what Jesus did and how he did it, we can make fresh discoveries about his beliefs, values, and priorities.

"Symbolic conduct" is the term coined by David Perkins, Ph.D., of Harvard University, to describe how our behaviors communicate our attitudes, assumptions, and values:

> Our symbolic conduct and side messages have an often unseen but significant impact on the behavior of those around us. . . . Even though we may think we are just going about our ordinary affairs, even though we do not mean to send sweeping messages with our actions, inevitably the messages are often there. People read our behavior "between the lines," interpreting our behavior for its broader motives, attitudes, and commitments.[3]

There is a great deal we can learn by reading Jesus' behavior during the action-packed three-year period during which he trained and worked with his disciples, teaching multitudes of people, discussing religious law, confronting hypocrisy, and healing the sick. During all his activities, conversations, and preaching, Jesus conveyed much through words and much through symbolic conduct. You can be certain that your children read between the lines of your behavior to discover your true values and priorities and how you see them and feel about them.

> To understand the Good News and what it is, we have to not just listen to what Jesus says, but watch the way He lives. Most of His messages are hidden in His lifestyle, and particularly in the way He treated people.
>
> Joseph Girzone

Whatever your faith or lack of faith, whether you've attended worship services all your life or never, your paradigm, your worldview, will be shaken if you seriously commit yourself as a parent and as an individual to emulate Jesus. Jesus' teachings represent a new paradigm for thinking, feeling, worshiping, and interacting with others. They shocked the people of his time and shock us in ours. This doesn't mean that his example cannot be followed; it only means that we must first transform ourselves, as Stephen Covey would say, "from the inside out." If you do so, your child will inherit a lasting treasure: "To teach a child to love God and have Jesus as a friend and a role model in the way He treated people is to give a child a wholly different approach to morality. The child will still value the Commandments, but will now aspire to ideals far beyond the mere minimal requirements of the Commandments."[4]

PART 1

Our Inner Growth Comes First

"Therefore do not be anxious, saying, 'What shall we eat?' or 'What shall we drink?' or 'What shall we wear?' For the Gentiles seek all these things; and your heavenly Father knows that you need them all. But seek first his kingdom and his righteousness, and all these things shall be yours as well."

Matthew 6:31–33

Your Top Priority

Jesus wanted to know where each person's highest, most serious allegiance lay. Was it career, family, wealth, nation—or God?

One day a wealthy young man came up to Jesus, asking what good deed he must do to have eternal life. Jesus answered that he should keep the commandments. The man then asked which commandments in particular, and Jesus patiently recited six: "Do not kill, Do not commit adultery, Do not steal, Do not bear false witness, Do not defraud, Honor your father and mother" (Mark 10:19). The young fellow assured Jesus that he was already doing all that. But Jesus seemed to sense there was something lacking in this man's heart, for he then challenged him:

> And Jesus looking upon him loved him, and said to him, "You lack one thing; go, sell what you have, and give to the poor, and you will have treasure in heaven; and come, follow me." At that saying his countenance fell, and he went away sorrowful; for he had great possessions.
>
> Mark 10:21–22

"And Jesus looking upon him loved him." These words describe Jesus' approach even to strangers and his deep desire that everyone receive the benefits of a close relationship with God. If Jesus had raised *you*, what would he have taught as your first allegiance? In his actions and with every word he spoke, Jesus urged his followers to seek first God's kingdom and righteousness. The rest, he said, would follow. Philip Yancey writes:

> A society that welcomes people of all races and social classes, that is characterized by love and not polarization, that cares most for its weakest members, that stands for justice and righteousness in a world enamored with selfishness and decadence, a society in which members compete for the privilege of serving one another—this is what Jesus meant by the kingdom of God.[1]

And the rest *will* follow if you do likewise, as a parent and as an individual, no matter who you are or what your past has been. You may have been raised by wise, gentle people who sought first a genuine relationship with God; such parents seem to raise happy children quite naturally, imbuing their children with self-confidence and compassion for others. Perhaps your parents were different. If they didn't feel sure of themselves, were cynical about God or life in general, or suffered from problems that overwhelmed them, you may now doubt your ability to follow Jesus' teachings and example.

Whether you've felt blessed or unfavored until now, Jesus taught that it's never too late to ask God for help, forgiveness, or a fresh start. Even when the disciples made mistakes or disappointed him, Jesus made it clear that they were *still* chosen and could *still* become the leaders he knew they could be.

Take the Narrow Gate

In business, measurable goals and results are the focus. In Jesus' ministry, unmeasurable character and mental and spiritual transformations were the focus. When you choose Jesus as your role model, you cannot help but grow personally, which will transform you as a parent. In so doing, you are taking the most challenging path in life, the one that leads through what Jesus called "the narrow gate": "Enter by the narrow gate; for the gate is wide and the way is easy, that leads to destruction, and those who enter by it are many. For the gate is narrow and the way is hard, that leads to life, and those who find it are few" (Matt. 7:13–14).

We are the most important people in our children's lives. If we just muddle through, complaining about our children when problems arise, we'll receive comforting validation—for rare indeed is the friend who will gently point out our own blind spots—but our connectedness, hence our influence, with our children will deteriorate. I've seen so many argumentative or self-focused parents complain bitterly that they were suffering—and they truly were—because their child was argumentative or self-focused! *Whatever you seek for your child, you must first achieve for your-*

> For all who consent to a long process of maturation, little by little their inner self is built up, without their knowing how.
>
> Brother Roger

self. We who care about our children's inner as well as outer lives need the kind of "heartseeing" vision and exquisite listening skills that Jesus modeled in conversations with his disciples and others. If we steadfastly strive to raise our child as Jesus would, we will develop these abilities and strengthen our connection with our child.

But first we must learn from Jesus as his disciples did. In a sense, *we* must become disciples. As a disciple—defined by *World Book Dictionary* as "a believer in the thoughts and teachings of a leader"—we must not only learn from what Jesus said but seek to become increasingly like him in our mind and heart, thus becoming *transformed.* Jack Mezirow, a pioneering scholar in transformational learning, has found that people who aren't merely learning more information but are actually *transforming* their ways of seeing, thinking, and acting go through a series of important phases, including the following:

1. They encounter a "disorienting dilemma"—whether an event or a realization. This dilemma causes them to feel dissatisfied with a mind-set or situation.
2. Self-examination then begins, often with feelings such as fear, anger, or guilt.
3. They begin to question assumptions that they have long taken for granted.
4. They begin to explore options for new roles, relationships, or actions.
5. They start planning a new course of action.
6. Next, they begin to gather the knowledge and skill to put their plans into action.
7. They begin to "try on" new perspectives, roles, and behaviors.
8. With each new effort, they build competence and self-confidence.
9. Finally, they reintegrate their newfound perspectives and ways of thinking and acting into their lives.[2]

As you read this book, allow yourself to go through each of these phases *in your own way and time*. Those who try to hurry change, particularly genuine internal change, often end up where they began—at their old status quo. A caterpillar must spend many weeks inside its little cocoon, changing in tiny ways that others don't yet see. But the long-term transformation is truly miraculous as the beautiful butterfly leaves its sheltered space. As you examine Jesus' approach to his disciples and others, and think through his teachings as they apply to your life as an individual and a parent, little changes will begin to happen inside you that others may not yet see.

Effects on You

The World's Approach	Jesus' Approach
You are confused when people give you conflicting advice, either rigidly clinging to one approach or waffling among many.	You welcome, even seek, diverse ideas and perspectives, comparing each with Jesus' charter to select those that fit.
You're expected to be perfect, always right.	You're expected to become increasingly humble, willing and able to admit mistakes.
You're expected to know all the answers, to be certain, decisive, and dominant.	You're never expected to know it all but to model curiosity, thoughtfulness, concern for a child's opinion.
You are vulnerable to the criticism of others who ascribe to a particular approach or method.	You consider criticisms, comparing them with Jesus' charter before changing your approach or method.
You're frequently stressed by an ongoing need to monitor or discipline a child; defiance and rebelliousness tend to increase over time.	You need more thought, communication, and planning with a young child than later on; parenting becomes easier over time due to a strong parent/child connection.
You are worried and feel helpless, watching as your child is exposed to the world's priorities: money, sex, power.	You are confident that you are teaching and modeling God's values as counterpoint to the world's priorities.
When problems arise, you suffer self-doubt, self-blame, regrets.	When problems arise, you have the assurance and comfort of knowing that you have followed Jesus' charter to the best of your ability.

It Takes Time to Grow and Change

You may strive to be the best parent, CEO, teacher, attorney, or grandparent you can be, but in God's eyes, you're an individual first. While today's culture commands you to hurry up, use all the right techniques, and find quick-fix solutions to every problem, the truth is that your child will benefit most if you *slow down and nourish your own spirit* before attending to his or hers. The first step toward developing the capacity to see and respond to your children as Jesus would is to set aside some time for yourself, with daily prayer and at least a few moments of quiet reflection. If you can, find someone with whom you can talk about the five chapters in this section devoted to your own inner life and character. Or record your reactions, feelings, memories, and concerns in a journal.

Remember, Jesus never promised overnight solutions. What he promised was lasting and deep transformation once we begin to act more like gardeners than professors, patiently watering and nurturing the seed of the kingdom of heaven within our heart. Author Alan Nelson notes:

> In John 15, Jesus tells us to abide in him in order to bear fruit. It is the abiding that is the process. . . . Our natural inclination is to focus on the fruit bearing. We read books, go to seminars, and listen to cassettes on better fruit bearing. What we need to think about is better abiding. When we improve the process, the fruit will come naturally.[3]

Before you can guide your children, you must incorporate Jesus' teaching and values into your own heart and mind. This will require a good deal of practice and the unlearning of old habits, which can be difficult indeed; habits are, by their very nature, resistant to change. In fact, if from time to time it *doesn't* feel difficult or even discouraging as you strive to exchange the parenting-as-usual that you learned from others for parenting-as-Jesus-would, you're probably not trying hard enough! But if you keep at it, giving yourself time and rewarding yourself for even failed efforts in the right direction, you'll find that Jesus' principles are beginning to become your own.

If you are truly committed to this quest, staying in the game even when nothing seems to be working, the payoff is that you'll begin, very gradually, to see, respond to, and guide your child as Jesus would. You'll notice a new cooperative attitude, more genuine conversations, and the sense that your connection is growing much stronger. And that's a great feeling.

1

The Call

"You have not chosen me, but I have chosen you."

John 15:16 KJV

The best-kept secret in the Scriptures is this: Jesus "parented" his disciples, illustrating through his words and symbolic conduct how to lead and guide those in our care, and how God leads and guides us (if we allow it). As we observe how Jesus mentored his disciples, we have a model for parenting our children that is radically different from contemporary models. Never before have our communities, at home and around the world, been more desperately in need of the higher level of spirituality, moral reasoning, values, and behavior toward others that Jesus offered humanity. Our families and all those we touch will be blessed if we answer the call to seek transformation in ourselves and those we love by continuing to ask the question, "How would Jesus raise a child?"

You want the best for your child, not merely what modern society has to offer—that's why you're reading this book. You're probably wondering now how Jesus *would* raise your child. For that matter, how would Jesus have raised *you?*

You may be a new or expectant parent, just beginning the journey and wanting to give your child the best possible start.

Or your child may be doing well, as far as anyone can see, and you want to help him or her become attuned to God and learn to avoid the dangers of the world. Whatever your situation, you sense that the priorities and values of this world are counter to what is really most important. You want more for your child and for your family. Even parents of gifted children can find themselves wondering if there's something lacking, despite the absence of any noticeable problems. Kristin and Dave's eleven-year-old daughter, Heather, is gifted academically, so for several years they've been working overtime to fund private schooling for her. Yet the following is the kind of conversation that has become the norm.

> Dad: Everything okay, Heather? Sorry I haven't been around much. . . . I've been working a lot.
> Heather: Yeah.
> Dad: So, how's school?
> Heather: Good.
> Dad: Are you making good grades?
> Heather: Yeah.
> Dad: Sorry I haven't been around much. I'm trying to save up money so we can move into a better house.
> Heather: Okay, Dad.
> Dad: Hey, what are you watching there?
> Heather: A new show.
> Dad: Good. Well, I'm going to my office for a while to do some work, so—
> Heather: Okay, Dad.

You can see that something is lacking. The world would never notice, but you do. The world would never care, but you do. The world could never know what's missing, but Jesus would. Whoever you are, and whatever your situation, one thing is certain simply because you're reading this. You want more for your children than what the world has to offer. You want to set them on the right path, to show them the way they should go, so that they can begin life on a solid foundation. You want to build your home not on shifting sands but on a *rock*.

I Have Chosen You

In classic works of literature, when the hero receives a call, he has a choice. He sees what he could achieve and how his life could be, but pursuing the call is his choice and his alone. In the same way, saying yes to God's call is the sign of something truly heroic in the individual. Paradoxically, only those strong enough to admit that they want and need guidance can accept the call.

Sometimes the call comes through something we see, hear, or experience that feels unsettling or new. Quite often the call comes and goes without our conscious recognition, quietly percolating inside us over months or years. When finally we hear it and say yes, we may not even remember what it was that initially inspired us. Sometimes, however, we feel an inner commitment the moment we encounter the call.

When we're called to do something special but don't yet feel special, we may ignore or refuse the call; we convince ourselves that our lives are just too, well, ordinary. Yet when Jesus called people to follow him, they were simply going about their ordinary lives, and the Gospels do not suggest that they felt at all special in the beginning. Indeed they *weren't* special in human terms. They had no political or economic clout, no inheritance or great achievements, and little or no formal education. They were just like thousands of other people out there, trying to make a living from one day to the next.

Then Jesus entered their lives. He called them, giving them a vision of what they would do some day—wondrous things like healing, teaching, and preaching, for which, quite frankly, they were not qualified. How strange this must have seemed. Why was he interested in them? What on earth did they have to offer? They were ordinary fishermen and tax collectors, not rabbinical students, physicians, or philosophers. Yet somehow Jesus helped them believe in themselves. In calling them, Jesus entrusted to them a sacred task. Though they could not have known it at the time, Jesus, through word and deed, would eventually transform their hearts and minds. They would never be the same again.

Learning from Jesus

Perhaps the reason the disciples achieved so much under Jesus' tutelage is that he didn't just tell them, he *showed* them. He was careful to behave in accordance with his values, even when under pressure or stress. Jesus taught then helped sustain changes in his followers by his consistent words and actions. He *taught* them how to become teachers, *spiritually guided* them to become spiritual guides for others, and *led* them in such a way that they too became leaders. As you read the following example, both *hear* what Jesus said and *observe* what he did. In so doing, you'll begin to develop the skill of reading his symbolic conduct—behavior intentionally used to communicate and teach—an interpretive skill that you can use throughout life whenever you're unsure how to respond to a specific need or problem as Jesus would.

When Jesus' mother and brothers came to the place where he was teaching because they were concerned about his well-being, he didn't argue with them, nor did he stop what he was doing and go with them:

> When his family heard about this, they went to take charge of him, for they said, "He is out of his mind." And the teachers of the law who came down from Jerusalem said, "He is possessed

by Beelzebub! By the prince of demons he is driving out demons" (Mark 3:21–22 NIV).

And his mother and his brothers came; and standing outside they sent to him and called him. And a crowd was sitting about him; and they said to him, "Your mother and your brothers are outside, asking for you." And he replied, "Who are my mother and my brothers?" And looking around on those who sat about him, he said, "Here are my mother and my brothers! Whoever does the will of God is my brother, and sister, and mother" (vv. 31–35).

From Jesus' words we learn that those who seek to follow his teachings and do God's will are our family, along with our flesh-and-blood family members. If a family member can't understand your efforts to follow Jesus' example, you may need to find others who do. Thus we can and should gather together with those who share our goal of parenting as Jesus would, for they are our family too.

Yet there's more that can be mined from this brief episode in Jesus' life. If you closely observe Jesus' symbolic conduct, you'll learn even more. One of the best ways to read his behavior is to notice what he did and especially what he *didn't* do, in contrast to what you'd expect of other people, or yourself, in the same situation. How would you respond if, while teaching a group of people about something very important to you, your family members came and stood outside the classroom, asking for you? Imagine how you'd feel when, a bit earlier, your family had come "to take charge of you" because they'd heard that some people were questioning your mental stability?

I don't know about you, but I would be hard put to hold onto my train of thought. Furthermore, I'd feel embarrassed, angry, hurt, and tempted to leave, giving those family members a reproachful look on the way out. But Jesus did none of this. He continued teaching, even with this awkward situation taking place. In fact he used the dilemma facing him as an opportunity to teach the lesson of who his real family was! Now this took courage. More than that it required three abilities that we can emulate in our parenting:

1. an acceptance of the weaknesses of others (in this case, his family's giving in to understandable fears)
2. a refusal to respond with impulsive anger
3. the habit of keeping his eye on the prize (in this case, completing the teaching he'd come to do)

These qualities can guide the discerning parent. When our child is driving us crazy, we can:

1. strive to accept, as Jesus did, that people, including our children, behave impulsively at times
2. refuse to lose our temper when they do
3. keep our minds on what's most important

Of course, we must adjust our behavior to the age of the child. A fifteen-year-old who is nagging you to take him to the mall can wait for you to finish talking on the phone with a discouraged friend, but a hungry, bored, or fussy baby must be attended to before completing that call (for both your sakes!). You may find still more lessons in this encounter that I haven't noticed. The point is to keep comparing and contrasting. What would most people do in that situation, and what did Jesus do (and not do) in similar situations? How can you apply this to yourself as an individual and as a parent to become more and more like him?

▶ **Lesson 1: You've already been called.** One day, Jesus decided to go to Galilee and told Philip, "Follow me." Philip went to his friend Nathanael and told him that he'd found Jesus: "We have found him of whom Moses in the law and also the prophets wrote, Jesus of Nazareth, the son of Joseph" (John 1:45). Now

Nathanael was—to put it nicely—a person who said exactly what was on his mind:

> Nathanael said to him, "Can anything good come out of Nazareth?" Philip said to him, "Come and see." Jesus saw Nathanael coming to him, and said of him, "Behold, an Israelite indeed, in whom is no guile!" Nathanael said to him, "How do you know me?" Jesus answered him, "Before Philip called you, when you were under the fig tree, I saw you." Nathanael answered him, "Rabbi, you are the Son of God! You are the King of Israel!" Jesus answered him, "Because I said to you, I saw you under the fig tree, do you believe? You shall see greater things than these."
>
> John 1:46–50

I like Nathanael. He wasn't even close to perfect, but he was honest. He didn't always use tact, and even if his jab about Nazareth was half joking, he comes across as rather opinionated. Nathanael had that rare ability to say what he thought while still listening to what others had to say. I can just picture him relaxing under the fig tree, none too eager to leave that nice spot to see what Philip was so excited about. Yet despite this initial unenthusiastic response, Nathanael was amazed that Jesus had seen him first (implying that the fig tree was quite far away or secluded from Jesus' location), but even more importantly, that Jesus had *seen* his true self.

One day much later, the disciples were talking with Jesus, whose words were loving, appreciative, and encouraging. Then he said something startling:

> If you keep my commandments, you will abide in my love, just as I have kept my Father's commandments and abide in his love. These things I have spoken to you, that my joy may be in you, and that your joy may be full.
>
> This is my commandment, that you love one another as I have loved you. Greater love has no man than this, that a man lay

down his life for his friends. You are my friends if you do what I command you. No longer do I call you servants, for the servant does not know what his master is doing; but I have called you friends, for all that I have heard from my Father I have made known to you. You did not choose me, but I chose you and appointed you that you should go and bear fruit and that your fruit should abide; so that whatever you ask the Father in my name, he may give it to you.

John 15:10–16

You chose *me?* each must have been thinking. *Wait a minute! I made the choice to follow this teacher; I distinctly remember the day I decided I wanted to learn from him, so I left my occupation and . . .* What a revelation! They were all sitting there not merely because of their conscious choices, but because *Jesus* had chosen *them.* Like the disciples, we may feel humbled and amazed at the thought that perhaps *we* didn't choose to seek God and learn how to raise our children as Jesus would, but that these very desires were gifts from God, callings to pursue a new path. This sense of being subject to divine selection, if you will, makes us take more seriously the longings of our heart and brings with it the realization that we have already been seen, pursued, even wooed by God.

▶ **Lesson 2: Many parents refuse the call.** Jesus told this story to help people understand that we may be called by God yet, for one reason or another, find ourselves declining the offer:

"The kingdom of heaven may be compared to a king who gave a marriage feast for his son, and sent his servants to call those who were invited to the marriage feast; but they would not come. Again he sent other servants, saying, 'Tell those who are invited, Behold, I have made ready my dinner, my oxen and my fat calves are killed, and everything is ready; come to the marriage feast.' But they made light of it and went off, one to his farm, another to his business, while the rest seized his servants, treated them shamefully, and killed them. The king was angry, and he sent his troops and destroyed those murderers and burned their city. Then he said to his servants, 'The wedding is ready, but those invited were not worthy. Go therefore to the thoroughfares, and invite to the marriage feast as many as you find.' And those servants went out into the streets and gathered all whom they found, both bad and good; so the wedding hall was filled with guests.

But when the king came in to look at the guests, he saw there a man who had no wedding garment; and he said to him, 'Friend, how did you get in here without a wedding garment?' And he was speechless. Then the king said to the attendants, 'Bind him hand and foot, and cast him into the outer darkness; there men will weep and gnash their teeth.' For many are called, but few are chosen."

Matthew 22:2–14

Jesus was making the point that when God calls us, whether to relationship with him or to a special task, we may say no simply because we don't realize what's at stake. In the case of parents, they may think their children are doing fine, hence there's no need to monitor their development or pray for their spiritual growth. When finally they realize their mistake, the children may have slipped far from them, or from God. It's so easy to get lost in the rush-rush pace of modern life. Refusing your calling is a risk both to you and your child—if you don't know where you're going, you'll end up somewhere else.

▶ **Lesson 3: No experience required, with opportunities for advancement.** Jesus didn't look for people who were already leading others;

> One day Alice came to a fork in the road and saw a Cheshire cat in a tree.
>
> "Which road do I take?" she asked.
>
> His response was a question: "Where do you want to go?"
>
> "I don't know," Alice answered.
>
> "Then," said the cat, "it doesn't matter."
>
> Lewis Carroll

41

instead, he called people who were busy making a living like everybody else. God does not expect us to already be parenting with confidence or great skill—though most of us are more experienced at parenting than those fishermen were at preaching! When Jesus called Simon (Peter), Andrew, James, and John, for example, they had no training or experience for the work that Jesus had in mind for them:

> As he walked by the Sea of Galilee, he saw two brothers, Simon who is called Peter and Andrew his brother, casting a net into the sea; for they were fishermen. And he said to them, "Follow me, and I will make you fishers of men." Immediately they left their nets and followed him. And going on from there he saw two other brothers, James the son of Zebedee and John his brother, in the boat with Zebedee their father, mending their nets, and he called them. Immediately they left the boat and their father, and followed him.
>
> Matthew 4:18–22

Jesus wasn't just asking these people to accompany him; he was asking each of them to become an *akolouthos*, or follower, of his teaching. He was asking them to come learn from him, to align themselves with his message. In so doing, they would acquire the knowledge, spiritual understanding, and experience needed to carry out the important tasks that Jesus would later assign to them.

▶ **Lesson 4: The more you learn, the more confidence and skill you'll have.** Only when Jesus' followers had internalized his thoughts, words, and behaviors could he give them the authority to teach and minister to others. When he gave them authority, he was giving them not just the permission but the confidence as well to go without him on their mission.

Although you may feel ready right away to begin putting Jesus' parenting techniques into action, Jesus taught that anyone seeking to guide and teach others must do some internal work first.

With each little bit of progress, however, you'll sense that God is granting you more authority and giving you more instructions to help your child in ways you'd never have thought possible. Jesus gave clear instructions to his followers for their new work, for he knew that they were new at this, and he didn't expect them to know what to do or how to handle difficulties along the way:

> And he called to him his twelve disciples and gave them authority over unclean spirits, to cast them out, and to heal every disease and every infirmity. . . .
>
> These twelve Jesus sent out, charging them, "Go nowhere among the Gentiles, and enter no town of the Samaritans, but go rather to the lost sheep of the house of Israel. And preach as you go, saying, 'The kingdom of heaven is at hand.' Heal the sick, raise the dead, cleanse lepers, cast out demons. You received without pay, give without pay. Take no gold, nor silver, nor copper in your belts, no bag for your journey, nor two tunics, nor sandals, nor a staff; for the laborer deserves his food. And whatever town or village you enter, find out who is worthy in it, and stay with him until you depart. As you enter the house, salute it. And if the house is worthy, let your peace come upon it; but if it is not worthy, let your peace return to you. And if any one will not receive you or listen to your words, shake off the dust from your feet as you leave that house or town."
>
> Matthew 10:1, 5–14

In raising his disciples to become mature leaders, Jesus didn't just "call 'em and leave 'em" but coached them over time. He didn't simply give motivational you-can-do-it speeches but was there for the long haul to instruct and encourage them daily.

▶ **Lesson 5: This is a long-term mission, not an overnight process.** When Jesus called the disciples, he didn't say, "Just do as you're told," or hype them up with promises of fast results, fame, or riches. He offered them a *long-term* vision of what they could become and achieve if they stayed true to that vision. He vividly described how even the smallest faith in God and one's calling can grow over time:

> Another parable he put before them, saying, "The kingdom of heaven is like a grain of mustard seed which a man took and sowed in his field; it is the smallest of all seeds, but when it has grown it is the greatest of shrubs and becomes a tree, so that the birds of the air come and make nests in its branches."
>
> He told them another parable. "The kingdom of heaven is like leaven which a woman took and hid in three measures of meal, till it was all leavened."
>
> Matthew 13:31–33

So it is with our own spiritual development as individuals *and* as parents. We cannot possibly hope to simply read a book and—presto!—begin parenting as Jesus would. The kingdom of heaven begins in our heart and mind "like a grain of mustard seed," which is tiny indeed. Jesus knew that those wanting to follow his teachings in order to experience this new inner kingdom would quickly get discouraged and quit trying if they expected huge changes overnight. So he emphasized again and again how even one little seed can take root and grow over time into something beautiful and grand. We must recognize that we will learn, and our children will benefit from what we learn, over time. This is a long-term mission, not something that we can check off our appointment books as we complete each step. In a world that pressures us to hurry up and suggests shortcuts of all kinds, Jesus' teachings stand apart, requiring that we slow down and focus on the *lifelong process* of becoming more and more like him, as individuals and as parents.

▶ **Lesson 6: You will have to make some sacrifices.** Jesus warned those who wished to follow him that they would have to make sacrifices. For instance, he said that people must go so far as to put the call to follow his teachings ahead of their family (the word *hate*—in Greek, *miseo*—as used in the following passage, meant to give one thing a lower priority or preference than another. In this context it did *not* mean to despise, as we use the word *hate* today[1]):

> Now great multitudes accompanied him; and he turned and said to them, "If any one comes to me and does not hate his own father and mother and wife and children and brothers and sisters, yes, and even his own life, he cannot be my disciple. Whoever does not bear his own cross and come after me, cannot be my disciple."
>
> Luke 14:25–27

Jesus stressed that following him—striving to become more like him—means traveling a long and difficult road, passable only by those with the strongest commitment:

> As they were going along the road, a man said to him, "I will follow you wherever you go." And Jesus said to him, "Foxes have holes, and birds of the air have nests; but the Son of man has nowhere to lay his head." To another he said, "Follow me." But he said, "Lord, let me first go and bury my father." But he said to him, "Leave the dead to bury their own dead; but as for you, go and proclaim the kingdom of God." Another said, "I will follow you, Lord; but let me first say farewell to those at my home." Jesus said to him, "No one who puts his hand to the plow and looks back is fit for the kingdom of God."
>
> Luke 9:57–62

Sounds like a lot to ask, doesn't it? Those who became part of Jesus' traveling ministry did leave their families behind. But even Jesus visited with his family and friends from time to time. What he was saying here had more to do with priorities, for if people weren't willing to leave their former lives, they'd never become invested in this challenging new mission. For parents, it's not as counterintuitive as it may seem to place our families below our calling to follow Jesus' teachings. If we do not do this, there will always be little problems and big crises distracting us, making us forget what's most important. If we give our calling top priority, our children will *always* benefit, for we will be raising them according to Jesus' principles rather than our own habits, impulses, or sheer guesswork.

▶ **Lesson 7: Be open to change internally as well as externally.** Jesus knew that his teachings were new, even revolutionary, yet he wasn't trying to undo religion or religious laws. Rather, he was calling for a deeper, internal commitment to their spirit and initial intent: "Think not that I have come to abolish the law and the prophets; I have come not to abolish them but to fulfil them" (Matt. 5:17). Marcus Braybrooke notes that many Christian scholars, in light of Jesus' criticism of some attitudes held by the Pharisees, "think Jesus' loyalty to the Law is surprising. But a growing number of scholars now regard Jesus as a pious Jew who dutifully kept the Law: Jesus was not undermining it, but completing it, by calling for more radical and inward obedience to God."[2]

> No one sews a piece of unshrunk cloth on an old garment; if he does, the patch tears away from it, the new from the old, and a worse tear is made. And no one puts new wine into old wineskins; if he does, the wine will burst the skins, and the wine is lost, and so are the skins; but new wine is for fresh skins.
>
> Mark 2:21–22

In Jesus' day, wine was stored in wineskins rather than bottles. When these skins were new, they were somewhat pliable, but as they aged, they became hard and stiff. New wine, still fermenting, releases gases that cause pressure. Barclay notes that "if the skin is new it will yield to the pressure, but if it is old and hard and dry it will explode and wine and skin alike will be lost. Jesus is pleading for a certain elasticity in our minds. It is fatally easy to become set in our ways."³ One simple event—being accepted and appreciated by Jesus—spurred great internal *and* external changes in a greedy tax collector who nonetheless proved to have a pliable, teachable mind and spirit:

> He entered Jericho and was passing through. And there was a man named Zacchaeus; he was a chief tax collector, and rich. And he sought to see who Jesus was, but could not, on account of the crowd, because he was small of stature. So he ran on ahead and climbed up into a sycamore tree to see him, for he was to pass that way. And when Jesus came to the place, he looked up and said to him, "Zacchaeus, make haste and come down; for I must stay at your house today." So he made haste and came down, and received him joyfully. And when they saw it they all murmured, "He has gone in to be the guest of a man who is a sinner." And Zacchaeus stood and said to the Lord, "Behold, Lord, the half of my goods I give to the poor; and if I have defrauded any one of anything, I restore it fourfold." And Jesus said to him, "Today salvation has come to this house, since he also is a son of Abraham. For the Son of man came to seek and to save the lost."
>
> Luke 19:1–10

If we think we know it all, we cannot say yes to the call because our certainty blinds us to our need to learn and grow. Jesus taught that those who wish to enter the kingdom of heaven must be new, not only on the outside, but on the inside— where know-it-all attitudes often abide—as well:

> Jesus said, "For judgment I came into this world, that those who do not see may see, and that those who see may become blind." Some of the Pharisees near him heard this, and they said to him, "Are we also blind?" Jesus said to them, "If you were blind, you would have no guilt; but now that you say, 'We see,' your guilt remains."
>
> John 9:39–41

47

As we seek to parent our children as Jesus would, we must acknowledge that we don't know it all before we can receive God's wisdom. Certainty is the enemy of change, as Jesus well knew. It can be hard to let go and consider new ideas, but if you are called and have said yes to that call, you can do it.

▶ **Lesson 8: When you hear the call, expect a blessing.** At Jesus' baptism, he received a blessing revealing God's pleasure and confidence in him: "When all the people were being baptized, Jesus was baptized too. And as he was praying, heaven was opened and the Holy Spirit descended on him in bodily form like a dove. And a voice came from heaven: 'You are my Son, whom I love; with you I am well pleased'"(Luke 3:21–22 NIV).

"You are my Son, whom I love; with you I am well pleased." What wonderful words these were for someone who was about to embark on a mission! When we are called to do something far beyond anything we'd once hoped to achieve, we may feel overwhelmed. This is why feeling blessed by someone is so important; it gives us fuel to begin our journey. Our blessing can come through another person's words, through seeing something that triggers a calling in us, or as a whisper in the recesses of our own heart. In whatever way we receive it—and we are wise to remember this when we want to support our child in something new—*the blessing accompanies the call.* We are blessed when we sense the call to transform ourselves and our families. Though we may not see how right now, God favors us and considers us capable of achieving our new mission.

Called to Raise a Child as Jesus Would

Jesus' emphasis on the call and our response to the call has enormous implications for us as parents. When we bring a child of any age into our life—whether our biological, foster, or adopted child, our spouse's child by a former relationship, our

48

niece, nephew, grandchild, or any other child—we are embarking on a sacred journey. After all, what could be more important to God than the nurturance and guidance of a new life? Yet we're not accustomed to thinking of raising children as a profoundly spiritual undertaking. In busy, money-driven cultures around the world, child rearing isn't referred to with the same respect and admiration as, say, career advancement opportunities or today's stock market report. While it's assumed that parents love their children, hanging out with the kids just doesn't seem a very profitable way to spend one's time.

Not only is parenting not given a high place in the popular culture, it is often considered nothing but a liability. Some would argue that since children are born to teenagers and others ill-equipped for parenthood, there are some parents who just don't qualify as being called or blessed. Yet God can and often does call us when we do not feel ready. Jesus said that what is impossible with men is possible with God (Matt. 19:26). But sometimes the mother or father isn't ready for the call.

For instance, I've worked with many grandparents who felt called to raise their grandchild because their teen or young adult child could not handle the responsibility. Such grandparents are a blessing to their children and their grandchildren, despite the conflicts that are common in these situations. Months or years later the child's parent may return or mature, yet the child has become accustomed to seeing his or her grandparent as a parent. Making it through these difficult times requires a lot of courage and patience on all sides. But more than anything, it requires faith in God's ability to see, beneath the conflicts and hurt feelings on all sides, a glimmer of what both parent and

> The role of parents is a unique one, a sacred stewardship in life. Is there really anything that would outweigh the importance of fulfilling that stewardship well?
>
> Stephen Covey

grandparent truly are inside, and even more important, what they can yet become to one another.

A parent—defined here as anyone who has responsibility for raising a child—can say yes to the call only if he or she is willing not to know it all and is thus able to receive God's wisdom and help. Parents who have attained considerable career or financial success are naturally more at risk for assuming that they know all there is to know, which often results in alienated rich kids who aspire to nothing more than achieving ever greater status and popularity than their peers or who see their parents as walking wallets or insensitive strangers. These men and women, despite being called, have not answered with a yes, because they already know everything there is to know about parenting.

How Will You Answer?

Some people seem to be called quietly, and they accept it without delay. Others discover their calling, whether in terms of vocation or parenthood, only after some problem or struggle. In *The Verdict* Paul Newman plays a self-loathing, alcoholic personal-injury lawyer who's been eking out a meager living as an "ambulance chaser," cynically approaching grieving relatives in the hope of getting a lawsuit to fund his next drinking spree. Finally, his life falls apart, and out of pity his friend gives him a small malpractice case. Newman' character goes through the routine steps, interviewing relatives and obtaining medical notes, then goes to the nursing home to take photos of the brain-dead young woman whose case he'll represent. She's curled in a fetal position, tubes and machines keeping her body alive, a woman whose future was destroyed by someone's carelessness. His camera clicks off the required photos when, quite suddenly, he really *sees* her.

> He has half the deed done who has made a beginning.
>
> Horace

For a heart-stopping moment, we see through his eyes. We feel his icy cynicism and apathy fall crashing to the floor. We know that he will now seek justice, even with all the cards stacked against him, not for the money but to honor this young life and for justice itself. Out of the pit that his life had become, this man has been *called*.

This is the kind of calling—the kind we don't see coming—that many parents experience. For some, the call to go beyond the norm for one's child occurs when he or she develops a physical or emotional illness. For others, the call is heard when their child has problems at school or has a friend with a drug problem. Some parents feel called when their child begins to show a special talent or gift, while others are called when their child is growing more emotionally distant. What matters isn't *when* we hear the call, it's *that* we hear it and answer yes to it.

This being said, keep in mind that there will be days when you feel neither called nor chosen. Like Tevye of *Fiddler on the Roof,* you may wish that God would choose you a little less often! Take heart in knowing that those days merely signal that you've become discouraged, overtired, or overwhelmed by responsibilities, challenges, or hardships. When you don't feel acceptable as a person or as a parent—let alone blessed or chosen—recognize this as your cue to take some time for rest and prayer. We have all been there. Sometimes our children present us with complaints or problems we never anticipated. Sometimes their words or actions hurt us. We then may get stuck in blaming, hurting, or kicking ourselves. These responses are not helpful to you or your child. Jesus was often exasperated with his disciples or tired or both. In following his example, you must forgive your human weakness and refresh your spirit through quiet time and prayer. Pray for a renewed sense of this most vital vocation for which you have been

> The significance of a man is not in what he attains but rather in what he longs to attain.
>
> Kahlil Gibran

51

chosen. Remember, if a person had to be perfect to be chosen, the disciples would not have been, and neither would we.

Remember and Reflect

How did you see yourself most of the time as a child? Did you ever feel called—whether or not you would have used that term—to do something special with your life, something, whether large or small, in a way that only you could do it? Or did you feel lost, unnoticed, and not at all special?

If you did sense that you had something special to offer to the world, what was it? Did you tell anyone about it? If not, why not? If so, how did they react?

In what ways do you feel that you and your family are on the right path?

What have you noticed in your child that makes you feel happy and blessed?

What things concern you? What would you like to change?

What does your child need that you would now like to provide for him or her, if only you felt called to do so and knew how to do it?

How might you, your child, or your whole family be different if you made the changes you dream of making?

How would Jesus help you to believe in yourself and your calling more deeply, as an individual and a parent, at this time in your life?

2

Servant Leadership

"Let the greatest among you become as the youngest, and the leader as one who serves."

Luke 22:26

Jesus wanted his disciples to become humble leaders who would rely on God's wisdom and strength and seek God's praise rather than the admiration of others. Only the leader who finds ways to serve others can hope to genuinely influence their hearts and minds. This chapter will describe Jesus' model for servant leadership and consider ways in which parents can follow that model to protect, guide, and influence their children as Jesus would.

In our modern mythology, leaders are tough. They rely on no one, make decisions quickly, and are always right. They give the orders; they know what's best. Many of our business and political leaders have public personae that say, *Unlike you, I'm the best and deserve extravagant pay and star treatment. I'm never wrong, so do as I say without question.* For worldly leaders— those leading for ego and greed, not for others—service is for servants. For them, gaining external power, control, and, above all, respect is the name of the game.

Jesus, tempted in the desert by visions of influence and power, had to make a decision about what kind of leader he would become.

If any man has a vision, his immediate problem is how to turn that vision into fact; he has to find some way to turn the dream into reality. That is precisely the problem that faced Jesus. He had come to lead men home to God. How was he to do it? What method was he to adopt? Was he to adopt the method of a mighty conqueror, or was he to adopt the method of patient, sacrificial love?[1]

Parents too must make a choice between ego leadership and servant leadership, for the two methods lead the family in opposite directions.

Many will ask, and it's a good question: But how can a parent serve? Your child is naturally immature and lacks the judgment of an adult. He or she may be in an angry or troubled phase, which means that you may be feeling angry or troubled yourself. Surely you need *more* control, not less! If this is the case, you don't want to become even more of a doormat than you already are. Even if you have the calmest toddler or easiest teen on earth, the thought of serving may initially sound foolish or irresponsible.

Fortunately, all these concerns can be put to rest, for Jesus did not mean by "serving" anything even close to becoming a doormat or catering to someone's every whim. Rather, what he wanted to see in his disciples was a sense of responsibility for those who would eventually look to them for leadership. Jesus understood very well the cycle of watch-imitate-become. Just as children *watch* their parents, *imitate* their behavior, and eventually *become* like them, so people would watch-imitate-become under the disciples' leadership. He certainly didn't want to train a group of people who would perpetuate the very behaviors he

> **When the best leader's work is done, the people say, "We did it ourselves!"**
>
> Lao-Tzu

56

spoke against! Hence he urged them to model themselves after *him,* not the typical bossy, haughty leader. Anybody can be a petty dictator. Jesus wanted his followers to become something far more powerful than that.

Learning from Jesus

When you think of leaders, what image comes to mind? What makes great leaders great? Leaders are portrayed in the media as decisive, tough-minded, proud, and self-sufficient. Their achievements inspire us, their "nerve" enthralls us; how we wish we could be like them! They shine like stars, and that is what we call them.

Yet we must ask what is real and what is air-brushed fantasy. For many, their influence is as fleeting as their fame. They call the shots as long as they can, but the minute someone else grabs the spotlight or wins the election, their leadership ends.

As parents who seek to raise our children as Jesus would, we can and must do better. A child in our modern culture is exposed to a multitude of influences every day, many of them harmful or even deadly. To offset the negative influences, you must develop the ability to wield influence of your own. You will do so if you learn to lead as Jesus did. *You can't use worldly methods to get heavenly results.* As we will see, Jesus recognized that typical leadership offers temporary control over others' behavior, but servant leadership leads to lasting influence on hearts and minds.

▶ **Lesson 1: The greater your service, the greater your influence.** Jesus *served* his disciples by teaching and carefully modeling servant leadership, rather than using a command-and-control model or leaving them to their own devices. He went to a lot of trouble to help them develop their leadership skills because he had such high hopes for them. Jesus knew that service is the path to influence. His followers, however, had trouble getting used to this idea. More than once, Jesus had to redirect them from worldly sentiments to a more service-oriented stance:

> And when it grew late, his disciples came to him and said, "This is a lonely place, and the hour is now late; send them away, to go into the country and villages round about and buy themselves something to eat." But he answered them, "You give them something to eat." And they said to him, "Shall we go and buy two hundred denarii worth of bread, and give it to them to eat?" And he said to them, "How many loaves have you? Go and see." And when they had found out, they said, "Five, and two fish." Then he commanded them all to sit down by companies upon the green grass. So they sat down in groups, by hundreds and by fifties. And taking the five loaves and the two fish he looked up to heaven, and blessed, and broke the loaves, and gave them to the disciples to set before the people; and he divided the two fish among them all. And they all ate and were satisfied.
>
> Mark 6:35–42

"You give them something to eat." Wait a minute! Why should they have to serve the public in such a menial way when they were being trained to become leaders of a great ministry? We parents sometimes ask ourselves the same kind of question. When we hold our newborn for the first time, we do not envision a room littered with toddler toys, getting up in the middle of the night when our child is sick, or listening to a teenager's laundry list of gripes. Yet service lies at the heart of parenthood, just as service was central to discipleship.

It must have been discouraging when Jesus heard his disciples arguing about who was the boss. How he must have yearned to hear them speak with the noble words of a servant leader, not the pitiful pleas of worldly power seekers: "Respect me! Honor me! Obey me!"

> A dispute also arose among them, which of them was to be regarded as the greatest. And he said to them, "The kings of the

Gentiles exercise lordship over them; and those in authority over them are called benefactors. But not so with you; rather let the greatest among you become as the youngest, and the leader as one who serves. For which is the greater, one who sits at table, or one who serves? Is it not the one who sits at table? But I am among you as one who serves."

Luke 22:24–27

But Jesus was not going to stop making his point about servant leadership until his disciples—who would soon be representing him and his message—understood that service is the hallmark of the greatest leader. So, since they couldn't seem to shake their ego and power obsessions, Jesus did something totally unexpected:

Jesus, knowing that the Father had given all things into his hands, and that he had come from God and was going to God, rose from supper, laid aside his garments, and girded himself with a towel. Then he poured water into a basin, and began to wash the disciples' feet, and to wipe them with the towel with which he was girded. He came to Simon Peter; and Peter said to him, "Lord, do you wash my feet?" Jesus answered him, "What I am doing you do not know now, but afterward you will understand." Peter said to him, "You shall never wash my feet." Jesus answered him, "If I do not wash you, you have no part in me." Simon Peter said to him, "Lord, not my feet only but also my hands and my head!" Jesus said to him, "He who has bathed does not need to wash, except for his feet, but he is clean all over; and you are clean, but not every one of you." For he knew who was to betray him; that was why he said, "You are not all clean."

When he had washed their feet, and taken his garments, and resumed his place, he said to them, "Do you know what I have done to you? You call me Teacher and Lord; and you are right, for so I am. If I then, your Lord and Teacher, have washed your feet, you also ought to wash one another's feet. For I have given you an example, that you also should do as I have done to you. Truly, truly, I say to you, a servant is not greater than his master; nor is he who is sent greater than he who sent him. If you know these things, blessed are you if you do them."

John 13:3–17

This action, considered suitable only for servants, must have made a deep impression on the stunned disciples. He certainly couldn't have made the point any clearer than that! In so doing, he also demonstrated that he was a leader who had the humility, strength, and integrity to "walk the talk." As parents, we too must practice what we preach and embed Jesus' teachings into our everyday lives. We must take care not to lord it over our children—as do those who parent by mood rather than principle—even if experts or religious leaders say it's okay. As Jesus said: "For I tell you, unless your righteousness exceeds that of the scribes and Pharisees, you will never enter the kingdom of heaven" (Matt. 5:20).

▶ **Lesson 2: When you *see* your child, that's servant leadership.** As will be seen in the chapters that follow, Jesus was acutely perceptive. He saw not just words or behaviors but the feelings that gave rise to them. He had a tremendous capacity for empathy. For instance, when he saw a grieving mother, he identified with her and felt compassion for her. Not only was her emotional loss terrible, but in those days a widow who had lost her only son could be facing a precarious future as well.

> As he drew near to the gate of the city, behold, a man who had died was being carried out, the only son of his mother, and she was a widow; and a large crowd from the city was with her. And when the Lord saw her, he had compassion on her and said to her, "Do not weep." And he came and touched the bier, and the bearers stood still. And he said, "Young man, I say to you, arise." And the dead man sat up, and began to speak. And he gave him to his mother.
>
> Luke 7:12–15

Jesus tried at every opportunity to help others see people as he saw them, rather than through society's judgmental or indifferent lens. Hear him as he describes to Simon, point by point, those actions and characteristics of this "lowly" woman that make her lovable, even admirable. Jesus' goal here was to model and teach an empathetic, compassionate attitude:

One of the Pharisees asked him to eat with him, and he went into the Pharisee's house, and sat at table. And behold, a woman of the city, who was a sinner, when she learned that he was sitting at table in the Pharisee's house, brought an alabaster flask of ointment, and standing behind him at his feet, weeping, she began to wet his feet with her tears, and wiped them with the hair of her head, and kissed his feet, and anointed them with the ointment. Now when the Pharisee who had invited him saw it, he said to himself, "If this man were a prophet, he would have known who and what sort of woman this is who is touching him, for she is a sinner." And Jesus answering said to him, "Simon, I have something to say to you." And he answered, "What is it, Teacher?" "A certain creditor had two debtors; one owed five hundred denarii, and the other fifty. When they could not pay, he forgave them both. Now which of them will love him more?" Simon answered, "The one, I suppose, to whom he forgave more." And he said to him, "You have judged rightly." Then turning toward the woman he said to Simon, "Do you see this woman? I entered your house, you gave me no water for my feet, but she has wet my feet with her tears and wiped them with her hair. You gave me no kiss, but from the time I came in she has not ceased to kiss my feet. You did not anoint my head with oil, but she has anointed my feet with ointment. Therefore I tell you, her sins, which are many, are forgiven, for she loved much; but he who is forgiven little, loves little."

Luke 7:36–47

Jesus' ability to *see* people made him dear to many. Looking past one's own concerns and feelings to see those of others is a sacrifice, something that few bother or remember to do. As parents, we too can become heartseeing. The most confident and attached children grow up trusting that adults really see them, notice and care about what they're experiencing, and can be counted on to soothe them when they're distressed. This happens through "mirroring": If the baby makes a sad face, the parent makes a sad face too, reflecting it back to the baby as a mirror does, but then makes soothing sounds to assure the tot that the parent *knows* he or she is sad and that everything's going to be all right. Once the child is old enough to understand, the parent adds a third step, called "sharing adult mastery,"[2] saying things like "Poor thing, I know you're feeling cranky, but that's because you got too tired at the park." In this way, the child's needs for safety and nurturance are served because he or she feels understood and helped through the confusion and overwhelming emotions.

Needless to say, this is easier for a parent if he or she was "mirrored" as a youngster. Those who were never seen in this way may have to learn and practice it quite deliberately. If you need help developing this kind of seeing, by all means get it. You might first try reading some of the books listed at the end of this book. For many people, this will open their eyes to the ways in which they've hungered all their lives to be truly seen by their parents and others and will help them develop their own heartseeing abilities. For others, parent group counseling or individual therapy will be necessary because there are too many old hurts inside or because they simply don't know where to start. Sometimes it's easier to unlearn old habits and try new things when you have a supportive friend or professional helper on your side.

As a supplement to these activities, I also recommend observing parents who have the qualities that you'd like to develop. This is something I did when my first child, Sascha, was young. I realized that I was, and had been from childhood, too hyper, busily racing around with college and work and all of my other responsibilities. Thus I had trouble slowing down to really see my daughter. A woman from my church took care of Sascha in the mornings while I went to class, and I noticed that her tempo was altogether different. She had that quality I wanted to develop, the ability to sit still while calmly listening to a child, really paying attention. *I wanted that.* So I observed her, taking mental notes. After a while, I felt myself changing. True, I was still the hyper type, but I learned how to control it when I was with Sascha, to see and hear her more clearly.

I was helped in this quest by watching the Public Television show *Mr. Rogers* with my children. Fred Rogers was so calm and patient that watching him helped me to slow down, stop doing a million things at once, and spend some quiet time with my kids. This, in turn, helped me to become more heartseeing and attentive. I encourage you to watch parents who have the heartseeing gift (though they may be hard to find!) and to watch positive models of heartseeing people on television or video. One such video is *Sister Act 2,* which portrays a hostile, confused teenager whose hardworking single mother loves her but can't really *see* her. Then one day a sensitive teacher sees her true longings and helps another teacher see the child. That teacher then tries to help the mother see the girl's longings. Heartseeing is something we must help one another with, for the person closest to the child often has the most trouble really seeing him or her. Becoming heartseeing is challenging but central to Jesus' leadership style and his ability to influence others.

▶ **Lesson 3: When you ease your child's suffering, that's servant leadership.** Jesus served the people who came seeking his help through a concrete act of love. He healed their physical and mental suffering, and in so doing, he bandaged up their spiritual wounds as well, offering them his love and acceptance. Some of those he healed were outcasts, rejected and scorned due to their illness or poverty, while some were Roman officials or wealthy citizens; Jesus made no distinctions along these lines. Though overwhelmed at times by all those seeking his help, he put his own needs aside to heal many people, including:

- the "madman" who lived among the tombs
- the paralytic dropped through the roof
- the woman who touched the hem of his garment
- Bartimaeus, the blind beggar
- the epileptic boy
- the man who had suffered an illness for thirty-eight years at the pool of Bethesda
- the woman with the crooked back
- the man with the withered hand

In serving these and many more through his compassion and his healing work, Jesus won their trust and proved his concern for their well-being. When we help those who are suffering, whether physically or emotionally, we win their trust. And people who trust their leaders are not only willing to follow them, they *want* to. You've probably nursed a sick child through a long dark night or comforted a tearful teenager after rejection or failure. Though they may not have said so in words, they felt gratitude that you were there and that you were willing to lay your own needs and wishes aside long enough to ease their suffering.

How did Jesus do his healing work? On close examination of the Gospel accounts of his healings, a pattern emerges in terms of initial introduction, diagnosis, and treatment. Though the details vary from incident to incident, the steps in his approach to the suffering person went something like this:

1. He *saw* them.
2. He *empathized* with what they were feeling, identifying with them.
3. He *asked* why they were speaking or behaving as they were.
4. He *diagnosed* the cause.
5. He effectively *responded* to each person's need.

This sequence is not unlike that used by good therapists and medical doctors:

See → Empathize → Ask → Diagnose → Respond

Healing may involve curing a current condition or diminishing the suffering associated with it. Parents do this all the time without realizing it. When we notice that our child looks troubled but isn't saying so, we usually go through some of these steps. We may ask what's wrong, and if he or she says, "Nothing," we go back to our computer or our cooking. Or we may imagine what's wrong and try to diagnose the cause. Sometimes we see a troubled look and respond without bothering with the middle steps, leading to some irritating or humorous situations for the child (for example, aspirin and chicken soup "prescribed" for what turns out to be lovesickness, not the flu).

We can serve by easing suffering, but only if we go through all five steps, which give maximum attention to the child's internal state and his or her own view of the problem with minimum guessing on our part. The next time you sense suffering in your child, friend, or spouse, try this five-step process. Keep tabs on how well you performed each step, and you'll begin to develop the finely tuned perceptiveness that Jesus displayed again and again.

It's important to note that sometimes it's difficult to get a child to open up or communicate clearly his or her needs, which makes diagnosing and responding to the cause of the problem difficult or impossible. At such times, we may need to talk with other parents, the child's teacher, or a pediatrician or counselor. By asking for help, we are serving our child's needs by caring more about his or her well-being than about appearing to "know it all." This requires that we accept the fact that every parent needs help now and then, especially when we're worried and "too close to the problem" to see the whole picture.

▶ **Lesson 4: When you take care of your child's practical needs, that's servant leadership.** Jesus took care of the little things:

- He told his disciples how to multiply food to feed the hungry crowds who had come to hear him teach.
- He told Jairus and his wife, after bringing their daughter back from the brink of death, to give her something to eat.
- He prepared meals for his disciples and reminded them to rest.
- He turned water into wine at the wedding in Cana to spare the hosts embarrassment when they ran out early in the evening.
- He helped the fishermen, who would later become his disciples, with their fishing, telling them where to find the biggest catch.

Jesus modeled a caring approach that didn't differentiate between big and little needs; he never told anyone that his or her needs were insignificant. Parents can better guide their children on the big issues when they've first helped them with the little things.

A psychologist friend of mine looked exhausted one morning, saying he'd been up all night building a soapbox car for his son. When I asked him why he did this, knowing he had a full day of clients scheduled, he said, "I want him to listen to me, but *I* didn't listen to *him*. I thought I was listening, but I guess I let him down when things got busy. So I didn't realize today was the deadline. If he missed it, he'd be disqualified for the race he's been waiting for all winter." He sighed heavily, looked at his watch, then said, "Hey, if we want them to care about what *we* have to say, we've got to care about what's important to *them*. So I'll be tired all day, but our relationship is worth it."

▶ **Lesson 5: When you defend your child from judgment or harm, that's servant leadership.** Our job as parents is complex; we want to protect our children, but we don't want to be overprotective. Sometimes we become aware that our child is being bullied, teased, or harshly criticized by peers. We are even more concerned when we discover that our child is being cursed at, threatened, or hit, especially if the person causing the harm is an adult. We naturally want to defend our child, but we may fear that we'll be hurt ourselves or that we'll lose our temper. These two fears tend to coexist and may paralyze us into inaction just when our child needs us most. Yet these are not the only choices for handling conflict, as we will see in chapter 9.

Jesus provided an excellent model for one of the most important forms of service that a parent, or any leader, can offer—the service of defending vulnerable people from judgmental criticism, injustice, or cruelty.

- He defended the blind man by stating that he was blind through no fault of his own nor because of his family's sins (common beliefs at that time).
- After healing the madman, Jesus defended him by sitting and talking calmly with him, thus sending the message that the man was worthy and capable of a place in society.
- He defended the woman accused of adultery, for which she would have received capital punishment, by saying, "If any one of you is without sin, let him be the first to throw a stone at her" (John 8:7 NIV).
- He defended the woman who anointed his hair with oil when others criticized her.
- Jesus defended the parents his disciples were shooing away, saying, "Let the children come to me" (Mark 10:14).
- He defended Zacchaeus by dining with him, despite others' concerns that visiting a tax collector was bad for public relations.

- Jesus defended the blind beggar Bartimaeus by stopping to talk with him, despite the urging of others to ignore him and press on with their journey.
- He defended the woman at the well from her own self-judgment by not dwelling on her past, instead asking her to drink the "living water."
- Jesus defended the poor and oppressed with cautionary tales regarding critical or merciless people. For example, he told the stories about poor Lazarus languishing outside the door of the uncaring rich man and about the man whose large debt was forgiven but who wouldn't forgive someone else's far smaller debt.

Clearly Jesus was a defender. Through these actions he proved himself genuinely caring, trustworthy, and courageous—qualities that could not help but inspire others to see and trust him as a leader.

▶ **Lesson 6: Knowing when to shift gears is a hallmark of servant leadership.** Servant leadership encompasses all forms of leadership, because it requires that we shift gears as our child's needs or conditions change. Dr. David Perkins and Daniel Wilson of Harvard University, in discussing intelligent organizations, note that any of four leadership approaches may be needed at a given time.[3] I've added parenting applications:

1. *Answer-centered leadership:* You issue commands and explain or answer, rather than ask questions or invite your child to come up with ideas, opinions, or plans. This is how we tend to lead in a crisis situation that doesn't allow time for discussion. For parents: This feels safe to a child and is required in some situations ("Don't touch the stove," for example). However, it doesn't help children learn or develop problem-solving skills and encourages dependency.

2. *Question-centered leadership:* You ask questions, seeking others' ideas and feedback and allowing everyone some input into decisions or problem-solving. For parents: This works best when things are fairly calm; it encourages the child's learning. If it's done well, it's perceived by the child as trusting, concerned, and fostering his or her development.

3. *Vision-centered leadership:* You provide a vision for the future. This approach inspires others to think and act but doesn't work if they don't know how to carry it out or don't share that vision. For parents: This can work within a specific context, such as in planning and carrying out a camping trip.

4. *Leadership by leaving alone:* You leave them to figure things out for themselves. This can inspire autonomous people but may feel unsupportive to those who need more guidance and monitoring. For parents: This can feel liberating for children who are ready for some independence within a specific context (as when an adolescent asks to be allowed to monitor her own schoolwork as long as she makes good grades).

Servant leadership trumps any other form of leadership because you must be able to *discern and deliver the leadership approach your child needs in each situation.* Hence, the servant leader must develop the skills of all other kinds of leaders and on top of this must know *when to reach for which approach* in the "leadership toolbox." Consider the effectiveness of a parent who is learning servant leadership, compared to the typical parent who knows only one leadership style and must use it regardless of the child's needs or how the situation changes.

▶ **Lesson 7: To be great in your child's eyes, be humble in God's.** While dining at the home of Simon the Pharisee and his friends, Jesus noticed several people trying to grab the most prestigious seats. Seeing an opportunity to teach, he told a story about the honor that follows humility and the fall that follows pride:

Now he told a parable to those who were invited, when he marked how they chose the places of honor, saying to them, "When you are invited by any one to a marriage feast, do not sit down in a place of honor, lest a more eminent man than you be invited by him; and he who invited you both will come and say to you, 'Give place to this man,' and then you will begin with shame to take the lowest place. But when you are invited, go and sit in the lowest place, so that when your host comes he may say to you, 'Friend, go up higher'; then you will be honored in the presence of all who sit at table with you. For every one who exalts himself will be humbled, and he who humbles himself will be exalted."

Luke 14:7–11

Jesus said on several occasions that even *he* did not seek or act on his own power: "I can on my own authority do nothing; as I hear, I judge; and my judgment is just, because I seek not my own will but the will of him who sent me" (John 5:30). Trying to be top dog—or even speaking in those terms—was antithetical to all that Jesus stood for. Rather than brag about making lots of money, getting a promotion, or "beating the competition" at work or in your social or family life, express gratitude for what you've achieved, gained, or won *with God's help*. This conveys to your child the message that our good fortune, though we may have worked hard to achieve it, must ultimately be credited to God. This does two additional things, both important for your child's spiritual development as well as your own: It acts as a "brake" of sorts, such that you'll no longer honor any gains that you achieved at the expense of someone else, and it reduces your pride in times of success and your self-blame when things go wrong. When you tame your ego by giving credit to God for your successes, you also protect your ego by humbly acknowledging that your own faith can falter and that you can forget to pray for strength and wisdom, thus getting stuck or otherwise experiencing failure. Your child, listening to you, will learn to see his or her

70

gifts and strengths as finite, which protects the child from the development of an overblown ego as well as the pain of self-condemnation.

▶ **Lesson 8: When you take care of yourself, that's servant leadership too.** It's not a conscious choice, but somehow parents end up taking care of everybody but themselves. After a while, neither body nor soul can keep up with the pace. Something has to give, and it's usually the parent, the child, or both. Self-care may seem an unusual form of servant leadership, but it's a very important part of providing service. Jesus protected his own energy and spirit, just as he guarded the well-being of his disciples, as we will see in chapter 4. Neither he nor his disciples would have been able to serve through healing and teaching had they stretched themselves too thin. Saying no is essential to servant leadership.

One mother, asked by church and community members to produce their art projects because she was good at it, finally realized that she was tired: "I was also confused. *Lord, the more I try to follow you, to serve you by helping others, the more drained I feel.* Something wasn't right." Indeed it wasn't, and she started saying no to many requests—allowing her more time for her children's activities.[4] If you don't take care of yourself, you can't possibly serve your child's most important needs.

A New Kind of Leader

Even a brief glance at our society reveals that our greatest leaders—those remembered not for winning this or that battle or election or Emmy award but for influencing multitudes—have been those whose power came from a zeal for helping others. That is, they subordinated their own egos for the advancement of causes they believed in, rather than furthering their personal ambitions. Abraham Lincoln, Mahatma Gandhi,

71

Mother Teresa, and Rev. Martin Luther King Jr. were leaders who put everything they had, even their health and well-being, on the line for those whose interests they served.

You may want to become a leader, or you may already be a leader in your work, family, or community. You may yearn for the power to do great things—and to be loved and appreciated for what you do. These are natural desires that can channel your energies in positive or negative directions, depending on how you handle them. If you're a parent, you need sufficient power and knowledge to be a great leader for your children. But what *kind* of power, what *kind* of knowledge do you need? Even more critical for us and for our children is the question *What kind of leader do I need to be?*

Jesus asked his disciples to serve in many ways—sometimes in material ways, as when they fed the crowds or healed the sick, and sometimes in providing spiritual and community leadership. Over time their commonplace desires for external power were transformed into a most remarkable spiritual power—the ability to *permanently influence* the hearts and minds of others, not merely to *temporarily control* their words and behaviors. If you think back to those whose guidance you wholeheartedly appreciated, under whose supervision you never felt belittled, you will notice something. Those people provided some service to you. We all, children and adults alike, need leaders who aren't just on a power trip, but who put aside their own interests and needs to lead and encourage us. And this transformation from concentrating on our own needs to focusing on the

> If you want to be the greatest—I sure do—then become a servant and be like the youngest (Matt. 23:11 and Luke 22:24–27). If you want to be first—okay—be last and be slave to all (Matt. 19:30 and Mark 10:44). . . . Amazingly, God takes our most driving urges and redirects them.
>
> Alan Nelson

72

needs of others must gradually take root and grow in the individual who dares to parent as Jesus would.

Remember and Reflect

What kind of leadership did your parents use when you were growing up?

What effects, positive and negative, large and small, did their leadership styles have on your abilities, your self-confidence, your patterns of interacting with others?

How did their parental leadership styles affect your leadership style as a parent?

How might your child change now and in the future if you begin today to practice servant leadership as Jesus did? How would this change affect you?

How would Jesus help you shift your parenting approach to truly influential servant leadership? What would he consider your greatest challenges in making the change?

3

Jesus' Charter

"Take my yoke upon you and learn from me."

Matthew 11:29

From the Beatitudes, which kicked off the Sermon on the Mount with shocking reversals of worldly priorities and values, throughout the remainder of this component of Jesus' "charter," a portrait emerges of a new character, with new values, worthy of the kingdom of heaven. Jesus' teachings were an alternative to the legalistic approach to worship that was common in his day and that continues to plague many religious institutions today. This chapter will describe that character in some detail and will discuss the challenging new ways of thinking and behaving that are prerequisites for anyone who seeks to raise a child as Jesus would.

We can refer to the sum total of all of Jesus' teachings, conveyed by word and deed, as Jesus' charter. Jesus required that his disciples learn and practice what he taught them, changing their own attitudes and behaviors before attempting to teach others. He required that they learn and understand his teachings, not merely memorize or parrot them, and commit themselves to following those teachings with their whole heart and mind. Jesus wasn't naïve about human nature. He knew very well that we fallible, needy beings need a lot of time to transform our habitual perspectives, assumptions, and ways of doing things. Changing habits is more time-consuming and challenging than any other kind of change.

Yet changes *must* take root in us before we can pass them along to our children. Jesus taught that God judges us by what is in our heart and by how consistently we try, not in how often we succeed or do better than the next guy. God is pleased with even small steps in the right direction. Sometimes we don't even realize we're doing something new, but God has quietly "called" us through one of Jesus' teachings.

John, a busy physician in a group practice, was proud of his son Jason, but he hardly saw the boy anymore. Jason holed up in his room every day, playing angry-sounding music from the moment he got home to the wee hours of the morning when he fell asleep. *Probably just the way teenagers are,* John reassured himself. One morning during a worship service, John heard the beatitude "Blessed are those who mourn" as if for the first time. With a jolt, he became alert and realized that somewhere deep inside he *was* mourning, mourning because he'd been so busy for years that he no longer knew his son.

This realization led John to consult with me in family counseling. He said that there was an irritability and quick-tempered quality about the boy that hadn't been there before. John had tried not to notice; usually he'd joke around with Jason to cheer him up. Jason would mumble something, then close his door. By getting in touch with his own sadness about the disconnect between him and his son, John began to *see and hear* again. As painful as it was, he *saw* Jason's wrinkled brow and *heard* his unhappy sighs whenever he went to the kitchen to get something to eat, retreating quickly back to his bedroom.

John had suddenly *heard* one little beatitude, a beatitude that could start the ball rolling toward a much-needed change in

> To bring up a child
> in the way he should
> go, travel that way
> yourself once
> in a while.
>
> Josh Billings

him and in his relationship with Jason. If John mourned, no longer denying that which he didn't want to see, his options for helping himself and his family would increase considerably. Fortunately, he did just this. He admitted that he'd prioritized career over family simply because they'd become accustomed to a high standard of living, which required working overtime to pay the bills.

While recognizing this hard truth, John faced the challenge of knowing what to do. He didn't know where to start. *How would Jesus handle this?* he began to wonder. This question led him to realize that Jesus would know that Jason needed more time with his father to restore a badly frayed connection and that Jason's spirit was suffering in some way. John prayed for guidance. Then, on one ordinary night, John saw Jason going to the kitchen and knew he had to try something new.

John: Hey, Jason, whatcha doing?

Jason: Nothing—just getting a snack.

John: (following Jason toward his bedroom): Jason, is something bothering you? You've been looking a little down lately.

Jason: No, just hungry. (Going inside his room, Jason prepares to elbow the door closed. John reaches out gently, holding it ajar for a moment.)

John: Okay, maybe you're just hungry. But I'm concerned about you. I've noticed lately you're staying in your room, and maybe there's nothing wrong, but . . .

Jason: Look, I'm about to drop this bowl . . . (Jason pushes the door a little with his foot.)

John: I know, but before you close the door I want to say that maybe nothing's wrong, *or* maybe you don't feel like talking about it right now, but I do notice you seem a little down lately. Go, enjoy your snack, but listen, whenever you feel like talking, no matter what it is, Buddy, I'm here

for you. And even if I'm dictating notes, I *want* to be inter-
rupted, because when it's about you, it's that important.
Got that?

Jason (still juggling his drink and bowl of popcorn, looks at
his normally preoccupied father quizzically): Well, uh—
yeah—thanks. (Jason slowly closes the door, feeling something he hasn't felt for a while.)

Was this encounter a success? Is John following Jesus' charter? Can focusing on one little beatitude do any good when
there's so much John needs to learn and change? It's not fair
for me to ask these questions, since I know how the story ends.
But the answers are yes, yes, and yes. Consider how incon-
spicuously this process began. As John was nodding off during
the sermon that day, God called him through a teaching that
was exactly what he needed to hear. True, it hit John where it
hurt. And though he'd heard the beatitudes a million times, this
time he really *heard* them. This time he did "mourn," rather
than rationalize or deny. This modest little beatitude led him
to realize that if he would allow himself to *feel* his worry about
Jason and to *mourn* the loss of a once close relationship, *he
would be comforted*. That's the promise Jesus made, and John
was going to hold God to it.

In a sense, though, God held John to *his* promise to repair
his relationship with Jason. This one incident was only the
beginning; afterward, life went on as usual, and hostility or dis-
tance remained in Jason's demeanor. John was committed to
making this change, however, and prayed daily to have the
patience and the will to keep *seeing* Jason. Again and again he
used his "X-ray vision"—his budding heartseeing ability—to
look past flippant remarks or mumbled comments. Again and
again he invited Jason to go out to eat or to a sports event, to
take Jason rollerblading or to the beach or the noisy arcade.
Despite Jason's declining most of these invitations, John car-

ried through on his commitment. John began to cut back some expenses and then his work hours.

Over a period of months, Jason began to soften; now and then he went out with his dad, and when he realized that this was for *him*, that his dad really wanted to know what was going on inside him, he began to talk about his loneliness and feelings of rejection at school. When Jason talked, John listened. And after a time, when John talked, *Jason* listened. Their connection had been restored. It took determination and courage to keep trying to reach Jason, but this kind of "prodigal patience" is what raising a child as Jesus would is all about. As Charles Swindoll notes, "Recovering from extreme difficulties usually requires an extreme amount of time."[1]

Learning from Jesus

Each beatitude is a tiny jewel, containing far more than its size would suggest. The beatitudes and some of Jesus' concise statements that follow are often glossed over as merely "pretty" sayings. Yet this is a great mistake. These jewels of wisdom guide us toward the perspectives and "mental models" that Jesus taught and demonstrated. If we "try on" these new ways of seeing, thinking, and acting, we can, little by little, come to view and respond to our children as Jesus would.

▶ **Lesson 1: Like the disciples, you are invited to learn from Jesus' teachings and let God transform you.** "And they went into Capernaum; and immediately on the sabbath he entered the synagogue and taught. And they were astonished at his teaching, for he taught them as one who had authority, and not as the scribes" (Mark 1:21–22). Indeed, Jesus did not teach as the scribes did. He didn't base his words on precedent—what this or that authority had said—*or* demand that people follow his teaching. He believed in choice. Jesus *invited* people to learn

79

from him, not in a formal teacher-student manner but in an altogether new way. In this invitation to learn from a caring, humble teacher, and in words cherished by the weary and needy for centuries, one can almost hear the strains of a love song: "Come to me, all who labor and are heavy laden, and I will give you rest. Take my yoke upon you, and learn from me; for I am gentle and lowly in heart, and you will find rest for your souls. For my yoke is easy, and my burden is light" (Matt. 11:28–30).

Why would Jesus say that his yoke is easy and his burden is light? Even one glance at the Sermon on the Mount can create a sense of overload, because it covers so much ground. Yet Jesus' yoke—that which joins the individual to Jesus' ways of thinking and behaving—is easy because his teachings are offered "by invitation only." Never did Jesus wish to force his teachings on anyone, for forced learning is neither genuine nor lasting. Jesus' burden—the weight of responsibility we feel when undertaking any new task—is light because he wasn't throwing at people more rules and regulations that had to be obeyed. For all of us who are weary and burdened with problems or responsibilities, learning from Jesus provides us, as individuals and as parents, with the wonderful confidence—so rare in today's world of tragic headlines and dire warnings—that whatever happens, *everything will be all right*. What a joy to have, as the old hymn says, this "blessed assurance" that come what may, we will know we're on the right path. Working with the parents of children who have been in trouble with the law, I have noticed a huge difference between those parents who tried to follow Jesus' teachings and prayed for God's help and those who had no faith, no rudder, no basis for hope. The children sensed this. I've seen many teens and young adults who've eventually turned themselves around because of a parent's stubborn faith.

We shouldn't expect to be completely transformed now and forever after one emotional prayer session. This was precisely the mind-set Jesus discouraged when he used examples of gardening to describe the way spiritual growth occurs. Seeds grow in good soil. Our job is to remove the weeds that can choke out the flowers and prune the bad fruit or weak branches so that good fruit will grow. We must prune anything in us, no matter how or why it got there, that limits our spiritual growth and thus our ability to raise our children in the way we wish them to grow.

▶ **Lesson 2: The beauty of the Beatitudes brings out the best in you.** If you want to become more like Jesus as a person and a parent, the Beatitudes are a wise and easy place to begin. In the Sermon on the Mount, Jesus taught that God blesses individuals who strive to live in a manner that is pleasing to God. Taken as a whole, the Beatitudes reflect the kind of character that will receive God's blessings.

> Seeing the crowds, he went up on the mountain, and when he sat down his disciples came to him. And he opened his mouth and taught them, saying:
> "Blessed are the poor in spirit, for theirs is the kingdom of heaven.
> "Blessed are those who mourn, for they shall be comforted.
> "Blessed are the meek, for they shall inherit the earth.
> "Blessed are those who hunger and thirst for righteousness, for they shall be satisfied.
> "Blessed are the merciful, for they shall obtain mercy.
> "Blessed are the pure in heart, for they shall see God.
> "Blessed are the peacemakers, for they shall be called sons of God.
> "Blessed are those who are persecuted for righteousness' sake, for theirs is the kingdom of heaven."
>
> Matthew 5:1–10

These few teachings are dense with meaning; most of us could use some help teasing out their essence. As you read over the chart below, just imagine that you have begun today to align yourself increasingly with the characteristics in the left-hand column despite the cultural forces against these changes as represented in the right-hand column. How would these changes affect you? How would they affect your child?

The characteristic that Jesus said God would bless in us:	Jesus' promises if you follow them in "the real world":	The world's values and advice "in the real world":
Poor in spirit	When you are humble and teachable, not proud and a know-it-all, which is easier for the financially poor, you will enter the kingdom of heaven.	Toot your own horn. Greed is good. Never let 'em see you sweat. Money talks; poverty listens. He who dies with the most toys wins.
Meek[2]	When you're gentle, not harsh with others, you will inherit the earth.	Show 'em who's boss. You gotta be cruel to be kind. The good die young.
Mourning	When you mourn for your own and others' sufferings, and are not apathetic and uncaring, you will be comforted.	It's not my problem. She's just manipulating you. Get over it! Cry and you cry alone.
Hungering/thirsting for righteousness	When you seek to grow in righteousness, to become aligned with and please God, your prayers will be answered.	Life is short; get it while you can. Keep up with the Joneses. How to be a millionaire. There is no right or wrong.
Merciful	When you have mercy on others, you will receive mercy.	Some people don't deserve mercy. Force is all they understand. Respect me! Obey me!
Pure in heart	When you focus on God and what's good and don't dwell on evil or allow evil thoughts, you will see God.	Think about all the evil people out there and what they deserve. Revenge is sweet.
Peacemaking	When you strive to bring peace and do not enjoy or encourage discord or gossip, you will be recognized as a child of God.	Let 'em have it! Let it all hang out. Divide and conquer. Keep 'em on their toes. Human beings are naturally violent.
Criticized or persecuted in seeking righteousness, that is, "uprightness"	When you stay true to your quest, despite persecution, ridicule, or other obstacles, the kingdom of heaven will be yours—you'll come into the presence of God.	You can't fight the media. Don't be a martyr. Stop being "holier-than-thou." Accept it. That's just how kids/things are these days. Don't rock the boat.

82

"No one," said Jesus, "will take your joy from you" (John 16:22). "The Beatitudes speak of that joy, which seeks us through our pain; that joy, which sorrow and loss and pain and grief are powerless to touch; that joy, which shines through tears and which nothing in life or death can take away. The world has its joys, and the world can just as easily lose its joys. A change in fortune, a collapse in health, the failure of a plan, the disappointment of an ambition, even a change in the weather can take away the fickle joy the world can give. The greatness of the Beatitudes is that they are not wistful glimpses of some future beauty; they are not even golden promises of some distant glory; they are triumphant shouts of bliss for a permanent joy that nothing in the world can ever take away."[3]

▶ **Lesson 3: You must unlearn the old before you can learn the new.** Human beings have a hard time with change, particularly when people they know experience radical, psychological changes. Psychologists and organizational researchers have discovered that planned changes often fail because the person trying to change underestimated what's called the "organizational immune system"[4] or "psychological immune system."[5] We're all built for homeostasis, which is the maintenance of things as they are—the status quo. If we weren't, then, for example, whenever we got ready for bed, we'd have to go through a list of activities in our mind: brushing our teeth, finding our pajamas, choosing a washcloth, washing our face, and so on. If it weren't for our psychological immune system keeping our habits and routines intact, we'd be up all night trying to figure out what to do and when!

Hence this immunity to new things or changes serves a purpose. It causes trouble, however, when it short-circuits our goals. We want to lose weight but can't seem to overcome our immunity to change in the area of eating habits. We want to be more patient with our toddler but our "immune system" kicks in, preventing us from trying a new, calmer method for handling fussiness. It's tough to break through the homeostasis that usually serves us well but sometimes gets in our way. To do this, we need to unearth, examine, and discard negative beliefs and assumptions. Many people try to skip over this essential step, but they end up painting over old, engrained habits and beliefs with new behaviors and ideas. This doesn't work, and won't last.

Charles, a forty-two-year old electrician, was raised by an anxious mother and a highly critical father. He knew his dad loved him, but Charles never felt he measured up to his father's expectations. Worried that his daughter, Amy, could end up with low self-esteem just as he had, Charles is trying to help her in the only way he knows, by pointing out her faults, hoping this will cause her to "get off her rear." He often warns her that she'll never amount to much (thinking this will motivate her to get better grades) or that she'll never get a boyfriend if she doesn't stop "eating like a pig" (thinking this will inspire her to stop overeating).

Charles felt a pang of guilt when his sister finally spoke with him about his misguided efforts to motivate Amy through criticism and judging. He decided he should stop, but he soon found that breaking an old habit isn't easy. He made a New Year's resolution never to judge her again. He didn't realize, however, that he had within him a critical spirit that led him to hurt his daughter "for her own good." His self-imposed "gag order" was difficult to follow. He tried not to say anything to her, but this just made matters worse, for she assumed he was angry or apathetic toward her.

What Charles must do is go deeper to go beyond his failed attempts. First, he needs to ask God for forgiveness so that he can begin anew. He needs to talk with other parents about positive ways to guide and motivate children and unlearn his old parenting methods. He may need to talk with a therapist to come to terms with and forgive his own father's hurtful words that he'd always, like a dutiful son, rationalized or denied. How would Jesus guide Charles to heal Amy's wounds from all those judgmental words and win back her trust in him? Is this degree of change an impossible dream?

In *The Empire Strikes Back,* wise old Yoda is trying to teach his weary, pessimistic student, Luke Skywalker, how to use "the force." Luke has learned to move rocks, but now Yoda instructs him to use the force to lift his spaceship from the murky water. Luke takes one look at the size of this challenge and gives up: "Master, moving rocks around is one thing, but this is totally different!" Yoda emphatically responds, "No! No different! Different only in your mind! You must *unlearn* what you have learned!" In the same sense, many people have told me that trying to live according to the Sermon on the Mount is just too big a task for human beings. Going to worship services is one thing, but making all these changes—that is totally different! The answer to this is the same as Yoda's answer to his student. We have to unlearn what we have learned about what we can and cannot do.

Unlearning requires that we examine even our most taken-for-granted beliefs, question them, and discard them if they are inaccurate or not well thought out. When I was getting used to my laptop, it took me several days to unlearn the placement of the keys on my familiar old desktop computer. Some moves were so ingrained that I actually had to cover certain keys with tape so as not to hit them accidentally, erasing my work each time! So it goes with the challenging internal changes for which Jesus promised blessings and rewards in the Beatitudes. They will require that we "tape over" certain habitual ways of thinking and behavior so that we can begin to learn and use what Jesus taught. It may feel awkward at first, but if you inhibit your usual ways of thinking, feeling, and behaving, eventually you will find that Jesus' teachings are not impossible to incorporate in your life after all. Certainly any real change requires energy and determi-

> A cynic can chill and dishearten with a single word.
> Ralph Waldo Emerson

nation (not to mention patience with yourself as you're learning). William Shakespeare said, "Wisely, and slow. They stumble that run fast." Give yourself time to unlearn the old ways, as well as time to learn Jesus' new ways.

▶ **Lesson 4: Strive to be like God, not to be God.** "You, therefore, must be perfect, as your heavenly Father is perfect" (Matt. 5:48). In my experience, this one sentence has caused more angst than most words spoken by Jesus. We may desire to live a life of obedience but are discouraged by what seems an impossible command. Yet this reflects a misunderstanding of what Jesus was trying to convey. He made this statement after giving the Sermon on the Mount, when he entreated his followers to make many important changes in their lives. Surely he didn't want to give the impression that everything he'd just said was null and void, in that no one could possibly become as perfect as God.

I used to worry about this instruction. Then, after further study, I realized that Jesus *didn't* say, "So be as perfect as God." To say this would be to imply that we are on equal footing with God, with equal powers of perfection. Rather, what Jesus was urging his listeners to do was to take his teachings seriously and strive toward the ideal that God represents. In essence, he was saying, "I know that I am teaching you many new things and asking a lot of you, but please don't take one look, say it's too big, and give up, only to follow what appear to be the more doable or feasible ways of the world. You can't be perfect, for only God is perfect. What you can do is *strive without ceasing* to become more and more like your heavenly Father."

What a difference and what a relief! We can aspire to be perfect as God is perfect, but—like the riddle "How do you eat an elephant?" to which the answer is "One bite at a time"—we can do so only one step at a time. We can begin today to refashion ourselves, with God's help, bit by bit, according to Jesus' charter. We will be successful if we have the desire and the com-

86

mitment to keep working toward that goal despite inevitable mistakes, failures, and setbacks.

▶ **Lesson 5: Take some time to acquaint yourself with, or remind yourself of, Jesus' teachings.** Consider what Jesus taught in the remainder of his epic Sermon on the Mount. Its overarching themes are that those who please God *will surpass the righteousness* of even those who seem or claim to be perfect and *will go beyond what's required of them.* These requirements, which can be fulfilled even by those who behave hypocritically or with cruelty toward others, are found in the law, religious authorities, the world's standards and values, and even our usual priorities. The headline of Jesus' message was shocking and unambiguous: Anyone who wishes to enter the kingdom of heaven must *surpass and go beyond these standards.*

The sermon gives many basic guidelines to accomplish these overarching goals. I list them below in summary form. As you read them, check off those that you find relatively easy or are already doing. Even if there's only one, thank God and feel the joy of knowing that you've already begun striving to be like God. If you can't find any that you can honestly say you're doing now, simply pray for the commitment and strength to begin to change today. Seeking to become "perfect, as your heavenly Father is perfect," is a lifelong process. Remember, you can take your time and rely on God's ongoing help. After going through the following "character portrait," you'll have an idea of the main areas you'll need to work on *over time* for your child's sake, your family's well-being, and your own spiritual growth.

In your heart and mind, strive to:

- allow no anger to linger in your heart

> Character is what God and the angels know of us; reputation is what men and women think of us.
>
> Horace Mann

87

- actively remove desires that tempt you to behave in ways that you later regret
- reset your priorities, placing God before money
- keep your eyes on the good, not on that which feeds resentment or despair
- refuse to be anxious the way those with no faith in God are anxious

In your relationship with God, strive to:

- pray or fast in private, with humility and heartfelt words meant for God alone
- reconcile differences with someone before approaching God in worship or prayer
- ask for whatever you need from God in the confident way that a child asks his or her trusted parent
- enter by the narrow gate, seeking always the higher—and more difficult—path by following Jesus' teachings and seeking first the kingdom of God above all worldly things

In your relationship with others, including your children, strive to:

- not swear or call people names when you're angry
- not abandon your spouse or lust after others
- not resist or fight people with evil intentions
- love your enemies; pray for those who persecute you
- be generous to those who beg or borrow from you
- be friendly and respectful to everyone, not just your relatives and friends
- judge others as harshly or generously as you want God to judge you
- examine your own faults before addressing those of others

- avoid trying to teach those who aren't open to learning at that moment

When learning from other people while following Jesus' charter, strive to:

- beware of those who appear to be righteous, but aren't truly righteous deep inside where it counts
- evaluate people, especially experts and leaders, not by their position, money, education, or eloquent words but by their fruit: the human feelings and consequences to which their words and actions lead
- keep in mind that many call Jesus "Lord" but are not following his teachings
- hear and do Jesus' teachings, and your house will be built not on shifting sands but on a rock

Lesson 6: "Please be patient. God's not finished with me yet!" This is one of my favorite bumper stickers, and I imagine Jesus would approve of it. Do you suppose that Jesus, after delivering his sermon, expected his listeners from that moment on to be perfectly humble and merciful, to never judge anybody, to end all conflicts, and to bring peace wherever they went? Do you imagine that he considered them ready and able never again to harbor anger in their hearts? If he had, he wouldn't have urged them to pray regularly that God would not lead them into temptation and would forgive their trespasses. There would have been no need because they would have already arrived! Jesus knew very well that the new character he was defining was different from what people were accustomed to, not only in how they treated each other but in their attitudes, thoughts, and leadership styles as well. How could anyone live up to all that? Jesus knew that no human on earth could *live up to* that but that any person with a strong desire

and commitment could *be* living up to it. There's a big difference between striving for perfection and reaching it.

In the course of trying to reach a worthy goal, especially one
that involves transforming ourselves, it can be tempting to
behave as usual while changing on the inside. While internal
change is certainly essential, equally important is making sure
that our internal changes show up in our words and behaviors—our symbolic conduct toward others. We needn't, and
shouldn't, wait until we're "done"; remember, we will never
arrive at perfection in God's eyes. Let any positive change be
manifest in your daily life. It will not only benefit your child, it
will actually confirm in your own heart that you are changing.
Perkins notes: "One's symbolic conduct is a message to oneself.
The problem with principles is that they are not themselves
actions. . . . In sum, the messages one sends to oneself through
one's conduct can either reinforce long-standing paths of behavior or announce to oneself—and to others—new roads under
construction."[6]

Transformational change—the kind of change that Jesus
commanded his followers to undertake—is the most challenging of all, requiring us to alter not just the form and contents
but the *function* of our hearts and minds. To transform a business or a school means to change not only its external appearance but also its internal contents and ways of operating. Transformational change can sometimes happen quickly in a discrete
area, as when John's heartblindness toward his son, Jason, was
healed when he heard "Blessed are those who mourn" in a new
way. But system-wide transformation—transformation of one's
character, heart, and mind—happens only
gradually and with great effort.

Even those of us raised on the Scriptures
must learn how to apply Jesus' teachings
one step at a time. Don't try to process all
his teachings at one sitting, or you may get
mental indigestion or give up altogether.

> Whatever is good
> to know is difficult
> to learn.
>
> Greek proverb

Persevere in the areas that God reveals you need to change. When God sees that you have begun your journey in earnest, your blessings will begin. Life won't suddenly be a magic carpet ride filled with only good things, but, along the way, you will find yourself growing stronger, happier, and more confident as a person and as a parent. Your child will sense it too.

It can be challenging to realize that we have a lot of work to do on ourselves. Jesus' requirement, however, is to commit ourselves to the ongoing process of learning and practicing Jesus' charter, imperfectly and gradually. Like the disciples, we will begin to accumulate the knowledge and ability to help others—including our children—once we've made progress ourselves. And we can indeed pass along what we have learned if we do as Jesus instructed by making time daily for rest and prayer and regularly retreating alone or with others to commune with God. The next chapter will show you how.

Remember and Reflect

Which of your present *behaviors* are at least somewhat like those that Jesus taught and modeled? Which are not like his at this time?

Which of your *values and attitudes* toward others are at least somewhat like those that Jesus taught and modeled? Which are not like his?

When you were growing up, which values, attitudes, and behaviors in your parents and other family mem-

> Nothing great is created suddenly, any more than a bunch of grapes or a fig. If you tell me that you desire a fig, I answer that there must be time. Let it first blossom, then bear fruit, then ripen.
>
> Epictetus

bers were most like those that Jesus taught? Which did not conform to his teachings?

What changes would you most like to make to be more like the character that Jesus taught and modeled? What benefits will these changes bring to you and your child?

In what ways will your relationship with yourself, your child, and God be affected if you decide to make these changes? Which area of his charter would Jesus consider most important for you to work on today?

4

Taking Care of Yourself

And he said to them, "Come away by yourselves to a lonely place, and rest a while."

Mark 6:31

Many people assume that they "should" pray. Jesus taught that prayer isn't just something we're supposed to do, it's something we can do. Quiet, humble, childlike prayer in a restful moment is a lifeline for us and our children. This chapter will describe Jesus' prayer practice and his insistence that the disciples, though busy teaching, guiding, and healing other people, take the time to rest, pray, and restore their spirits.

Tradition has it that a Zen master was visited by a philosophy professor who was eager to learn from him. As the visitor began to ask many questions about the meaning of life and happiness and suffering, the master was pouring him a cup of tea. The professor continued to ask questions until he saw that the cup was overflowing and quickly alerted the old man that he should stop pouring. But the master kept smiling and pouring, until the tea ran over the table and onto the floor. "Are you mad? Can't you see that it's overflowing?" Finally the master stopped and said, "You are an intelligent man. But, like the tea cup, your mind is already full, so that nothing I say can enter. Sit back, clear your mind, and ask only when you are 'empty' enough to hear what I say to you."

How can we be taught, how can we be guided, how can we receive love and support if we come to God thinking we already understand ourselves or our child? To pray as Jesus taught and prayed, we must come to God as an *empty cup*.

Learning from Jesus

Children of every age need from their parents emotional support, practical help, and spiritual guidance. What a demanding job! Especially for single, low-income, or working parents, parents with physical or emotional illnesses, and parents caring for sick or elderly relatives, the normal needs of any child can drain what little energy is left over at the end of the day. Not surprisingly, we all fall short from time to time. We all take wrong turns or fail to see problems early enough to prevent bigger ones from developing. We all make mistakes.

The biggest danger for any parent, however, isn't making mistakes. The greatest hazard is *failing to see or admit our mistakes*, which happens when we dig in, work harder, and rely on our own strength instead of taking a time-out to seek God's guidance, love, and support. What we need is a higher power source, and prayer is the wiring.

▶ **Lesson 1: Rest and pray at least once a day.** Jesus himself needed ongoing help from God, and despite his many sacrifices for others, he took good care of himself and his disciples. He frequently withdrew with his disciples from the crowds so that he and his disciples could regroup, rekindling their connections with one another and with God. Once, while preaching to a large, pressing crowd,

> There are some people that if they don't know, you can't tell 'em.
>
> Louis Armstrong

Jesus pushed away in a boat to keep from being crushed, knowing that he had to take care of himself spiritually *and* physically to pursue his calling. "Again he began to teach beside the sea. And a very large crowd gathered about him, so that he got into a boat and sat in it on the sea; and the whole crowd was beside the sea on the land" (Mark 4:1).

Marcus Braybrooke notes: "Marriage and family life require enough time to nurture them. Those who seek out God or 'the meaning of life' need time for quiet contemplation. To achieve anything worthwhile and enduring—not least a satisfactory relationship with God—it is necessary, as the pearl merchant did, to make large sacrifices for the pearl beyond price."[1]

Jesus' symbolic conduct communicated the value he placed on prayer and rest, especially while in the midst of guiding and caring for others. One cannot help but feel amazement at Jesus' patience when his attempts to get some time alone were thwarted by people determined to reach him: "Now when Jesus heard this, he withdrew from there in a boat to a lonely place apart. But when the crowds heard it, they followed him on foot from the towns. As he went ashore he saw a great throng; and he had compassion on them, and healed their sick" (Matt. 14:13–14).

My own need for rest and solitude hit a new peak of desperation one night when I was twenty and my firstborn was two weeks old. After changing her, feeding her, rocking her, and doing everything else I could think of, she continued to scream. What had I done wrong? After a while I just cried along with her, wishing with all my might for just a few minutes of peace so that I could wash my hair. I'd never felt so frustrated and exhausted in my life. In desperation, I prayed silently, because I felt like such a failure as a mother. Not knowing what else to do, I prayed for help, specifically, to somehow become more like Jesus and less like me.

Prayer activates the subconscious in ways that researchers are only beginning to understand, and most of this research has been done in medical settings. But regardless of why or how, while praying amid the screams, I saw in my mind's eye an old church painting of Jesus. *How,* I wondered in my fatigue, *would Jesus interpret her cries? What would he do* now? Without quite realizing what was happening, I was getting "unstuck" from my miserable state. Looking at her unhappy red face, I wondered if I had what it took to be a parent. I took a deep breath and looked at her again, this time imagining I was looking at her through Jesus' eyes. *What if she isn't crying for a better mother?* as I had assumed in my youthful ignorance. *What if she's crying because she's so tired and uncomfortable and wants and needs me?* How would Jesus respond to this tiny, unhappy baby? I abandoned all hope for a shampoo, picked her up from her carrier and found that I was somehow calmer, able to tend to her as I imagined Jesus would. She cried a while more, but now I had the presence of mind to lay her over my knees, gently rubbing her back as I suddenly remembered—my mind no longer filled with self-focused thoughts—that this can soothe colicky babies.

This works! I realized, and from that day on, I didn't wait so long to pray when things were not going well. Rather than *ending* with the question, "How would Jesus respond to her right now?" I decided to make a habit of *beginning* with it. I encourage you to do the same. Asking this question will transform your relationship with your child, enhancing your ability to see him or her more clearly, and it will open your mind so that you can receive God's guidance and support. To bring this about, start viewing that *first moment* of frustration, worry, hurt, or irritation as a cue to take some time, even if only a few minutes, to pause and pray. Once your emotional reactions to your child automatically trigger prayer, rest, and asking how Jesus would respond in that situation, wonderful things begin to happen.

▶ **Lesson 2: Pray or fast alone with God.** When you pray for yourself or your child, make it *real.* Don't do it just because it

seems like the thing to do. We must avoid the common practice of praying or attending worship services to prove to others (or ourselves) that we're doing the right thing. Jesus, who
said that we should come to God with the humility and inno-
cence of a little child, warned against ostentatiously displaying
our piety in public to be seen and admired by others, which
reflects a misunderstanding of the nature of God.[2] One day he
told some haughty, condescending people a story about two
very different prayers, revealing very different motives:

> He also told this parable to some who trusted in themselves that
> they were righteous and despised others: "Two men went up
> into the temple to pray, one a Pharisee and the other a tax col-
> lector. The Pharisee stood and prayed thus with himself, 'God,
> I thank thee that I am not like other men, extortioners, unjust,
> adulterers, or even like this tax collector. I fast twice a week, I
> give tithes of all that I get.' But the tax collector, standing far off,
> would not even lift up his eyes to heaven, but beat his breast,
> saying, 'God, be merciful to me a sinner!' I tell you, this man
> went down to his house justified rather than the other; for every
> one who exalts himself will be humbled, but he who humbles
> himself will be exalted."
>
> Luke 18:9–14

Jesus emphasized God's preference for simple, childlike
prayers that involve no posturing. Neither, said Jesus, should
prayers involve a lot of flowery, oft-repeated phrases that come
from memory, not the heart:

> "And when you pray, you must not be like the hypocrites; for
> they love to stand and pray in the synagogues and at the street
> corners, that they may be seen by men. Truly, I say to you, they
> have received their reward. But when you pray, go into your
> room and shut the door and pray to your Father who is in secret;
> and your Father who sees in secret will reward you.

"And in praying do not heap up empty phrases as the Gentiles do; for they think that they will be heard for their many words. Do not be like them, for your Father knows what you need before you ask him."

Matthew 6:5–8

▶ **Lesson 3: Pray as Jesus did, like a child to a loving parent.**
Whether we're four years old or ninety-four, to God we are children and always will be. We need comforting when we're worn out and guidance when we're headed down the wrong path. We need forgiveness and mercy when we realize we've let our children down, been too harsh, or neglected them in some way.

We're so much harder on ourselves than God is. Many parents who've come to me for counseling have listed their past parenting mistakes and nearly *demanded* that I show a judgmental attitude! We may be hard-boiled at work, but when it comes to our children, we tend to blame ourselves and despair when we realize we've failed in some way.

When you pray to God, speak as Jesus instructed, as to a Parent who can see *all* your talents and needs, a Parent eager to shepherd you away from dangers and toward spiritual growth: "Pray then like this: Our Father who art in heaven, hallowed be thy name. Thy kingdom come, thy will be done, on earth as it is in heaven. Give us this

> From his intimate life of prayer with God and from a prayerful searching of the scriptures, Jesus had forged the basic convictions that animated his life and ministry. Basic convictions about God as a loving parent and about love as the fundamental bond of human relationships were joined to an unshakable integrity that translated principle into action. . . . He dared to address God in such affectionate terms that probably many of his contemporaries would be shocked.
>
> Donald Senior

98

day our daily bread; and forgive us our debts, as we also have forgiven our debtors; and lead us not into temptation, but deliver us from evil" (Matt. 6:9–13).

▶ **Lesson 4: Free your mind from resentments whenever you pray.** Jesus taught that God will *always* forgive us and have mercy on us if we do the same for others, including, of course, our children. In the following instruction, Jesus gave more specifics, as well as promises, that are very interesting.

> Truly, I say to you, whoever says to this mountain, "Be taken up and cast into the sea," and does not doubt in his heart, but believes that what he says will come to pass, it will be done for him. Therefore I tell you, whatever you ask in prayer, believe that you receive it, and you will. And whenever you stand praying, forgive, if you have anything against any one; so that your Father also who is in heaven may forgive you your trespasses.
>
> Mark 11:23–26

When I found this passage that I had overlooked, I began praying as Jesus instructs, believing (or trying to!) that I've already received what I'm praying for and declaring that I had forgiven *every* person I'd ever held anything against, no matter the reason. Believing I'd already received what I asked for was difficult enough, for it flies in the face of the ingrained maxim, "Don't count your chickens before they've hatched," but it was even more difficult to forgive everyone. The ego strongly resists letting people off the hook. Try it yourself and see if you don't agree that it's hard to do. Over the course of even one day, we can find ourselves irritated or angry at any number of strangers, family members, or friends. The days pass, and we may not realize we're holding something against these people. But subconsciously the resentment is there, using up valuable mental space and energy, much like old files clogging a computer's memory, thereby slowing its processing or even freezing the screen.

Even tiny grudges weigh us down. And believe it or not, one person we can easily resent is our child. Maybe *resent* isn't quite the right word, but that feeling of not having gotten over a child's embarrassing tantrum or rude remarks is one that many parents will recognize. Such unreleased feelings can weaken our connection with our immature child, who can't or won't try to make amends. We must remember that *we* are the adults. No matter the age of our child, we parents are responsible for behaving in a wiser, more mature manner. Forgiving them (and everyone else who's wronged us) every time we pray will release us to begin again with the right attitude. We can't help our children better manage *their* feelings while we're focusing on ours. Over time this prayer practice became easier for me, just as it will for you if you begin using it daily.

▶ **Lesson 5: Anxiety is your cue to pray for whatever you need.** Jesus recognized the human capacity for anxiety. Unlike fear, which motivates a person to take some action to flee or overcome a threat, anxiety eats away at the human spirit.

Every parent knows about anxiety. We worry about our child's development, friendships, schoolwork, and spiritual life. We worry when we can't buy them things that their friends have or give them necessities that they deserve as much as any other child. We worry about drug use, violent television programming, and today's hypersexualized culture. Jesus warned against stewing and worrying about the future, which keeps us from improving those things over which we have control right now. He taught that we should seek first God's kingdom and righteousness, and the rest will follow:

> Anxiety is a thin stream of fear trickling through the mind. If encouraged, it cuts a channel into which all other thoughts are drained.
>
> Arthur Somers Roche

"Therefore I tell you, do not be anxious about your life, what you shall eat or what you shall drink, nor about your body, what you shall put on. Is not life more than food, and the body more than clothing? Look at the birds of the air; they neither sow nor reap nor gather into barns, and yet your heavenly Father feeds them. Are you not of more value than they? And which of you by being anxious can add one cubit to his span of life? And why are you anxious about clothing? Consider the lilies of the field, how they grow; they neither toil nor spin; yet I tell you, even Solomon in all his glory was not arrayed like one of these. But if God so clothes the grass of the field, which today is alive and tomorrow is thrown into the oven, will he not much more clothe you, O men of little faith? Therefore do not be anxious, saying, "What shall we eat?" or "What shall we drink?" or "What shall we wear?" For the Gentiles seek all these things; and your heavenly Father knows that you need them all. But seek first his kingdom and his righteousness, and all these things shall be yours as well.

"Therefore do not be anxious about tomorrow, for tomorrow will be anxious for itself. Let the day's own trouble be sufficient for the day."

Matthew 6:25–34

▶ **Lesson 6: Be a pest in prayer!** Jesus taught his followers to persevere and be determined in their prayers. He told stories about people who sought what they needed in a persistent, even bothersome, way:

And he told them a parable, to the effect that they ought always to pray and not lose heart. He said, "In a certain city there was a judge who neither feared God nor regarded man; and there was a widow in that city who kept coming to him and saying, 'Vindicate me against my adversary.' For a while he refused; but afterward he said to himself, 'Though I neither fear God nor regard man, yet because this widow bothers me, I will vindicate her, or she will wear me out by her continual coming.'" And the Lord said, "Hear what the unrighteous judge says. And will not

God vindicate his elect, who cry to him day and night? Will he
delay long over them?"

Luke 18:1–7

And he said to them, "Which of you who has a friend will go to
him at midnight and say to him, 'Friend, lend me three loaves;
for a friend of mine has arrived on a journey, and I have nothing to set before him'; and he will answer from within, 'Do not
bother me; the door is now shut, and my children are with me
in bed; I cannot get up and give you anything'? I tell you, though
he will not get up and give him anything because he is his friend,
yet because of his importunity he will rise and give him whatever he needs. And I tell you, Ask, and it will be given you; seek,
and you will find; knock, and it will be opened to you. For every
one who asks receives, and he who seeks finds, and to him who
knocks it will be opened. What father among you, if his son asks
for a fish, will instead of a fish give him a serpent; or if he asks
for an egg, will give him a scorpion? If you then, who are evil,
know how to give good gifts to your children, how much more
will the heavenly Father give the Holy Spirit to those who ask
him!"

Luke 11:5–13

Jesus encountered several people who persisted in their asking—for instance, the Greek woman who begged for "the
crumbs" of his healing abilities to heal her possessed daughter; the woman who secretly touched the hem of his garment
to be healed of her bleeding disorder; and Bartimaeus, the rau-
cously begging blind man who repeatedly asked Jesus to restore
his vision, even after others urged Jesus to keep walking on his
journey. Jesus modeled God's response to bold and persistent
prayer by helping each of these people, sometimes comment-
ing on their determination or cleverness in getting his attention and assistance. When you pray for yourself or your child,
don't be shy or worry about "bothering" God. Jesus made this
point in many ways. Pray for what is on your heart, as many

102

times as you need. God answers persistent prayer—though it may not be in the form or at the time expected—because the person who keeps asking God for help is a person with great faith.

Praying as Jesus Prayed

Someone once chastised me for praying with just one word—"Help!" He said this wasn't good enough, but it was all I could muster during that stressful period. Yet my experience, and that of many others, confirms that "Help!" can be quite sufficient. Certainly, if God knows what's in our hearts, as Jesus affirmed, we don't always have to put our thoughts and needs into words. We have only to calm our spirits and minds, pray regularly, and wait until we're able to perceive God's guidance. And to do this, we have to know ourselves well enough to recognize when we're headed for trouble and need to rest and pray.

When my cell phone is losing battery power, calls become less clear. The "low battery" sign flashes on the screen, warning that if I don't provide a time-out for recharging, it will soon stop working altogether. If I keep using the phone, it cuts off in the middle of conversations.

If we as parents had a "low battery" signal that clearly flashed before our eyes when our energy, patience, or wisdom was running low, perhaps we would get to God in prayer before finding ourselves in the middle of a crisis! If you're sensitive to your own inner signals, you may be adept at recognizing the subtle signs—irritability, indecision, sadness, or that rushed, overwhelmed feeling. But even for the most sensitive parent, these signs can be obscured by a host of other problems and demands on our attention. We may forget our priorities, spending our time putting out fires rather than preventing them in the first place.

If at first you don't succeed, pray, pray again.

This is why Jesus taught and modeled a prayer practice that includes three elements:

1. asking for God's help
2. withdrawing to a quiet place to listen for that help
3. resting physically and spiritually

This practice prevented both Jesus and his largely unschooled disciples from spreading themselves too thin, thus becoming exhausted or burned out.

The following are elements of Jesus' prayer practice.[3] Jesus prayed:

- alone, frequently; he withdrew
- often in early morning and at day's end
- spontaneously, as the need arose
- as he normally spoke, in his own words
- before making important decisions
- for himself and his "daily bread"
- for his disciples, friends, and others

You and your child will both reap benefits when you follow this teaching:

▶ **Benefit 1: Your physical and mental energy to play with and care for your child will increase.** The Gospels make it clear that Jesus and the disciples ministered to many people on a regular basis and naturally suffered from fatigue and stress. They needed daily "recharging." Modern parents may not be feeding crowds or healing the sick, but we too are constantly shepherding and nurturing people—our children. That Jesus had to remind his disciples to rest, eat, pray, and unwind suggests they might have neglected themselves at times in their zeal to serve. Many parents fail to safeguard their health, energy, and spirit. Your quiet time with God may reveal that you're weary or confused and that you need to recharge your emotional batteries, call a friend, make career or lifestyle changes, enter therapy, or join a parent support group.

▶ **Benefit 2. You will discover the best ways to guide your child.** When your child is having problems or getting into trouble, you may not know how to help. The listening, receptive form of prayer can provide you with a clearer idea of how to handle the situation. This practice also improves your empathic ability, helping you imagine what your child is feeling or struggling with. If you wish to handle your child's difficulties in a more positive way than you have in the past, or more effectively than your own were handled when you were young, the first step is to ask God for discernment, for that heartseeing ability that Jesus modeled.

▶ **Benefit 3. You will develop your ability to pause.** Taking a break, whether a long walk or a short bath, allows you to step back from noisy or stressful situations so you can think more clearly. Setting aside time for yourself helps prevent knee-jerk responses to misbehavior or other problems.

Stephen Covey writes:

What we all need is a "pause button"—something that enables us to stop between what happens to us and our response to it, and to choose our own response. It's possible for us as individuals to develop this capacity to pause. And it's also possible to develop a habit right at the center of a family culture of learning to pause and give wiser responses.[4]

> The real art of conversation is not only to say the right thing in the right place but to leave unsaid the wrong thing at the wrong moment.
>
> Dorothy Nevill

Covey describes a mother who was raised in a difficult home environment, but who is learning to do things differently with her own children:

> Now when I get into a frustrating situation, I pause. I examine my tendencies. I compare them against my vision. I back away from speaking impulsively or striking out. I constantly strive for perspective and control. Because the struggle continues, I retire frequently to the solitude of my own inner self to recommit to win my battles privately, to get my motives straight.[5]

When we remember to pray and take a short break—even if it's only in our mind—when we close our eyes and tune out the noise for a quick prayer, we'll have far more emotional clarity and will be able to pause before we speak or act.

▶ **Benefit 4. God will nurture you so that you are able to nurture your child.** Some parents give and give until they reach the burnout stage. But they can, by going to a lonely place or gathering with other parents for quiet prayer and reflection, become aware of this destructive pattern and take steps to rejuvenate their bodies and spirits. Like the in-case-of-emergency instructions given on airplanes that parents should give themselves oxygen before helping their child, it is essential that parents honor their own needs. It may seem selfish to ask someone to take care of your child so that you can go to a coffee shop, a park, or your back porch to rest, pray, and reflect, but this may do more for your child than hours of forcing yourself to be with him or her when you are physically or mentally exhausted.

▶ **Benefit 5. Early detection and prevention of problems will become possible.** Another benefit of following Jesus' prayer practice has to do with prevention. A parent who is taking the time to pray and listen for God's response is a parent whose vision is improved not only for today's problems but also for those that may lie down the road. In a sense, it gives us lead time. Our eyes are opened to what may happen if current patterns—such as a child's overly hectic schedule, eating habits, or behavior with friends—continue. An active prayer practice helps us see farther ahead so that *we* can act before *trouble* does.

▶ **Benefit 6. You will be able to identify a way to help when all else fails or it seems too late.** If your child is already facing difficult problems or seems lost in some way, you may wonder if it's too late to parent as Jesus would. The answer is an emphatic no! It's never too late to pray for our children and ourselves. Sometimes a child seems so angry, so disconnected from you, and so addicted to the wrong crowd or destructive values that you can't imagine a brighter future. Is there any point praying then? Jesus prayed even when things looked very bad for him, when he was surrounded by treachery, persecution, and betrayal. He modeled a close parent-child relationship with God in the face of death.

One mother I worked with in counseling was a tremendous inspiration because no matter the ups or downs that her son was going through, she always said, "I'm still praying, Dr. Whitehurst. All I can do is pray." This mother's stubborn devotion to God was mirrored in her stubborn devotion to her son.

As I worked with the family, I saw the power of that mother's prayers, for her son drew nearer and nearer to her over the years. When a child is at risk—or is already in serious trouble—we need to pray harder. We also need to enlist our friends and relatives, whatever their faith, in praying for him or her. Jesus told the story of the shepherd who left the ninety-nine sheep to go after the one lost sheep. Can we do any less for a lost child?

> You must *be* the change you wish to see in the world.
> Mahatma Gandhi

Annie's Story

Annie was constantly worried about her son Tyler's drug use. She knew that he was depressed and had tried everything, including medications and therapy. A therapist told her that she was overinvolved and needed to back out of Tyler's life. Yet whenever she did, his drug use worsened. Annie knew that something had to change. Yet backing out of his life felt wrong and risky as well. What else could she do? After speaking with a mother who had been there, Annie realized that she couldn't control Tyler's drug use. He went in and out of drug rehabs and psychiatric units, even jail cells. Annie was heartbroken; whenever I saw her, she tried to smile, but her sadness and fear were palpable.

Annie asked, "What more can I do? He does well for a while, then suddenly, like now, he's missing. I don't know where he is, what he's doing, or if he's alive. None of the doctors have been able to stop this addiction or the dangerous lifestyle that goes with it. I'm exhausted, and I see nothing more that I can do to save my precious boy." She burst into jagged sobs. She blamed herself, her husband, and sometimes God. "Tyler was such a good, sweet kid—how could this happen?" Annie felt relieved to express her anger at Tyler, the doctors, and the heroin dealers. I encouraged her to slow her breathing and to take a few moments to reflect on her child. He was more than an addict; he was a person who hurt so much that he turned to drugs for relief. And his own mother had no idea what the pain was about.

When a parent is afraid for her child, she wants to *do* something, to take immediate action. But some problems are bigger than we are. Sometimes going to a lonely place to pray, with or without others, is the very best thing we can do for our child. Jesus models for us a form of prayer that is anything but passive. Jesus prayed before he acted, before preaching to the crowds, and after the day's work was over. He prayed before making important decisions. In other words, he didn't stop at prayer; he *began* with it. What would Jesus do with a child like Tyler? First, he would spend time in daily, intensive prayer. He would invite others to join him in praying for Tyler. Jesus asked for company and support from others when his heart was filled with sorrow.

When Tyler called without revealing where he was, how would Jesus have responded? Jesus might well have waited for those calls just as Annie did, yet when he spoke to Tyler he would discern the degree to which Tyler felt detached and lost. Because he was heartseeing, Jesus would know that Tyler was not open to arguments for coming home or giving up drugs. He would perceive the need for connection above all else.

Annie began waking every morning at 5:30 to pray. She held an old photo of Tyler in her hand and prayed fervently for his safe return and escape from the heroin lifestyle. As the days and weeks passed, Tyler's calls became more frequent, and he sounded increasingly puzzled. Annie no longer argued with him about drugs, dangerous friends, or rebellious ways. Instead, she said, "Oh, Tyler, it's so good to hear from you. I love you and I'm praying for you. I've joined a parents' group, and they're all praying for you too. When you're ready to come home, we'll give you all the help and support you need."

As Annie changed, Tyler began to change as well. He began to realize that Annie didn't just care about his body or his criminal record—she cared about his heart, his inner being. And Annie no longer felt helpless and angry. Now she had something to do, something powerful that she could do every day for her son. She left her morning prayer sessions with a peaceful feeling.

One day Tyler appeared on her doorstep. Emaciated, unkempt, and despondent, he looked at Annie apprehensively. She threw her arms around him and brought him inside.

"Nobody knows the trouble I've seen; nobody knows but Jesus," as the beloved spiritual goes. When we get too tired, discouraged, or busy to pray, that is exactly when we need to stop and do it. Some argue that they can't pray as Jesus did because they're overwhelmed by problems that he never faced. How blind that is when you think about it. If anyone understood treachery, cruelty, apathy, and injustice, Jesus did. If anyone perceived evil and the suffering it inflicts on us and our children, Jesus did. If anyone would understand our desperate need for guidance, support, or even rescue, Jesus would. Jesus suffered as we do, and more, facing enormous pressure, criticism, and hatred from others. Yet through it all, he prayed with the confidence that God was with him always. And though we forget it time and again, God is always just a prayer away—*even at this very moment.*

Remember and Reflect

When was the last time you had significant time by yourself to rest and pray?

Parents can become tired, discouraged, physically sick, or clinically depressed. Are you able to accept help for yourself or your child when you most need it? Are you able to *admit* your weaknesses so that you can ask for help?

Are you isolated, or do you have friends who seek to raise their children as Jesus would? Where could you go and whom could you ask for help so that you can find a good support system?

Is your spouse on the same page when it comes to parenting issues? Do you both value spiritual as well as educational and physical development for your child?

Do you feel able to pray? Do you need help getting started in your prayer practice? Do you feel unfavored by God? Who could help you with these needs?

Are you able to get the rest you need so that you can "recharge your batteries"? If not, what needs to change? Is your work schedule unreasonable? Could your spouse, relative, or friend help you with child care?

Do you feel connected to God and able to ask him for anything you or your children need? What would Jesus say about your current pattern of rest and prayer?

5

Avoiding and Resisting Temptation

"Watch and pray."
Matthew 26:41

*The sobering reality is that the parent who seeks to follow Jesus'
charter in an attitude of servant leadership will face many temptations once he or she takes the heroic step of answering yes to the
call. As one comes closer to the good, the bad always raises its
head. In this chapter, we'll learn how to avoid falling into temptation, especially that which weakens our resolve and interferes
with our calling as parents.*

Popular culture considers it archaic, pessimistic, or a downer to
be on the lookout for temptation. We're exhorted in advertise-
ments, television commercials, billboards, and self-help books
to "think positive" and "don't worry; be happy." The idea of taking time out to examine one's thoughts and behaviors for flaws
is foreign to a success-oriented culture. Why would anyone actually *look* for ways in which he or she may be failing, making mistakes, or about to make a wrong turn? Spending time with such
negative thoughts, we assume, is a sign of depression, grim Puri-

tanism, or masochism. Yet keeping an eye out for temptation can accompany a joyful life and *keep* it joyful by warning us of detours or potholes ahead. While Jesus celebrated and enjoyed life with friends and strangers, he also watched for temptations that could weaken him or distract him from his mission.

Watching out for temptation as Jesus taught and modeled is by no means a heavy, dreary task. Through prayer and reflection, we can nip in the bud those thoughts or decisions that could lead to difficulties or pain. Jesus instructed his followers to watch and pray lest they fall into temptation, but he did *not* say, "Worry and pray," or "Expect the worst and pray." He simply said to watch, to keep our eyes open so that we can see temptations for what they are and keep them from causing problems for our children or ourselves.

Learning from Jesus

For parents, some temptations are simply givens. For instance, we must be strong and protective of our children, so we are tempted to lord it over them or become overly protective, stifling their development. We want to share our values with our children, but in the process we're tempted to talk too much and listen too little. We must set limits, but the temptation is to take advantage of being "the boss" to get our own way. Even good listening can bring its own clever temptation to be sympathetic but fail to give a needed push now and then to keep striving in the face of adversity. When it comes to parenting, the temptations are endless! Jesus taught his followers that they would be tempted in many ways, but he also taught them how to prevent or resist those temptations. We too can help our children and ourselves avoid giving in to temptations.

▶ **Lesson 1: Watch and pray every day to be able to see the temptations seeking out your child.** Jesus knew that temp-

114

tation comes to even the most devout, especially in times of stress or fatigue; he told the disciples at Gethsemane, "Watch and pray that you may not enter into temptation; the spirit indeed is willing, but the flesh is weak" (Matt. 26:41). Jesus taught and modeled that making time for self-reflection and prayer gives the individual "foresight," the ability to see temptation coming. This ability to see ahead is not limited to our own lives but can be used in an intercessory way for others as well, especially our children. Many parents have experienced the eerie intuition that tells them their child is in danger. But why not keep our channel of communication open to God *all* the time, rather than wait until problems develop? One mother taught me a valuable lesson in intercessory prayer that gave her the foresight to see that her son was headed straight into temptation.

This mother told me, "Dr. Whitehurst, I want you to help me get my son arrested." My face must have shown surprise, because Shandra quickly explained, "I've tried everything, but he just won't listen anymore. He's fifteen, but he's big for his age, and these older boys keep coming around and taking my James with them." Wringing her hands, Shandra looked like a small, frightened bird, sitting tensely on the edge of a large office chair.

Being new to the problems of the inner city, I asked why she would want him in jail. "Because I don't want him dead," was her simple reply. "These older boys are stealing and dealing drugs, and last week one of them got shot on his way to pick up James." She slumped over a bit, stared at the worn clinic carpet, and continued, "I know James's daddy whipped him when he was little, real strict, you know? Well, James was a sweet baby, and I know he's still sweet inside, but he started being angry all the time, and then he dropped out of school. He won't see a counselor; he's totally wild lately. And now, well, can you help me get him arrested? I beg him not to go with them, and I pray for him, but right now he just can't say no to those boys when they come around."

Shandra never cried a tear, but her jaw was set and I could see that she meant business. My heart went out to her. Imagine loving a child so much that you're willing to take his anger, even his rejection, just to buy him some time, time to grow up a little, time to separate from that deadly gang, and maybe, just maybe, gain the strength to resist temptations for quick riches, thrills, and—what James most craved and had never known—male acceptance. Of course, there are serious risks in placing a child in a juvenile center. If he is treated like an adult, he could easily grow into a hardened criminal. Yet on the streets James could lose his life. What would Jesus say to Shandra? How would he help her save her beloved son from temptation?

Shandra and I worked with a police officer who had spoken with her earlier. He agreed to speak to James and tell him that he'd end up in jail, or worse, if he didn't separate from that gang. This worked for a while, but James couldn't resist going out with the gang when they came around a month later. Shandra kept praying, and when one night her brother called from Georgia asking if she'd like James to come live with his family, her heart leapt with joy. Once away from the lure of the gang, and feeling the acceptance of his uncle, James turned his life around. The last I heard, he was attending vocational school.

Shandra, by watching and praying, had been able to see into the future, a future she wouldn't accept; her faith and determination helped her to save her son.

> **Every parent is at some time the father of the unreturned prodigal, with nothing to do but keep his house open to hope.**
>
> John Ciardi

▶ **Lesson 2: Your greatest temptation is to lose faith in God—to despair.** Jesus knew that losing faith in God—despair—leads to terrible things. Despair weakens the spirit of those who have suffered quietly or grieved over a child's problems and have never been able to tell their story or mourn with someone who cares. Jesus knew that when human beings encounter adversity or become fatigued, they can forget to pray and go back to relying on their own resources. Once this happens, despair sets in like a rude, uninvited houseguest.

In the midst of writing this book, I found myself unable to continue when the September 11 attacks occurred, followed by all manner of violence in Afghanistan, the Middle East, and elsewhere. This firestorm of fresh violence assailed me at every turn, whether I watched television or read the newspaper. I could not avoid hearing about whole families and countless young men suffering and dying around the world. We all have our Achilles' heel—that place where we are most susceptible to temptation—and mine had been struck. Despair slithered into my mind as I wondered who would care about raising children as Jesus would when people were so angry, hurting, and confused. Who would care about parenting children when the world was engaging in one "unavoidable" paroxysm of violence after another? For weeks I couldn't write; my spirit was weighed down. Though I prayed, my spirit remained hostage and my ability to hear God grew weaker. Along with millions across the world, I prayed for peace, but there was no peace.

Then one morning, during that first half-hour of the day that I devote to prayer, I heard a phrase in my mind, first soft, then louder, then so insistent that I had to write it in my journal: No matter what happens in the world, your mission remains the same. From that moment, I could write again. The world was in no better shape, but I was. And through praying daily as Jesus instructed, I finally received the renewed faith and courage I needed, and I knew without a doubt that *you*, my reader, were there, that *you* would care, and that God was calling you to raise your child as Jesus would—*now more than ever.*

> The man who is swimming against the stream knows the strength of it.
>
> Woodrow Wilson

117

Jesus came to a world that was in despair. . . . Men despaired of ever making themselves or the world any better. But with the coming of Jesus a new power came into life. He came not only with knowledge but with power. He came not only to show them the right way but to enable them to walk in it. He gave them not only instruction but a presence in which all the impossible things had become possible.[1]

Even while his enemies were gathering around him, Jesus prayed mightily for Simon Peter to be rescued from temptation's clutches, both for his disciple's sake and for those he would one day guide and teach. "Simon, Simon, behold, Satan demanded to have you, that he might sift you like wheat, but I have prayed for you that your faith may not fail; and when you have turned again, strengthen your brethren" (Luke 22:31–32). In his very next statement, Jesus predicted Simon Peter's three frightened denials of knowing Jesus, but this did not detract from Jesus' faith in him. Is this not remarkable? If Jesus were your parent and he knew that you would yield to some temptation—perhaps as serious as denying you were his child when the authorities came to arrest him—yet he said that he was praying for you so that your faith would not fail and that when you regained your strength you would strengthen others, how would that make you feel? Imagine such faith, such an understanding of your weaknesses, such belief in your gifts! How would it feel to be the recipient of that kind of love and faith?

▶ **Lesson 3: Pray to be kept away from temptation—in good times and bad.** Author Bruce Wilkerson makes the point that we are not limited to praying for help to resist temptation. He reminds us that we can pray that it be kept away from us in the first place.[2] In teaching his disciples how to pray, Jesus says to include, "Lead us not into temptation." Why resist evil when we can avoid it altogether? Certainly there are times when temptation seeks us out, but there are many more times when,

118

had we prayed for guidance, we might have avoided those dangerous situations in the first place.

When things are going well for us, our children, or our world, we naturally tend to become complacent. We stop paying attention or watching for potholes ahead. Wilkerson suggests that when things are running smoothly or going exceptionally well, we are wise to be proactive in praying for humility and protection from temptation: "Along with many others, I've discovered that the one time I'm particularly in need of this part [to be kept from evil] of Jabez's prayer is when I have just experienced a spiritual success. Paradoxically, that's when I'm most inclined to hold a wrong (and dangerous) view of my strengths."[3]

Needless to say, we are also apt to succumb to temptations of all kinds when we're worn out, frazzled beyond belief, and wondering how we'll get through the day. That's when we tend not to ask for help; hence, we can't very well receive it. Certain that we're alone in the world, we keep spinning our wheels in anxiety and worry, trying to do everything on our own power. While we *think* we're being rational, we're really succumbing to the most subtle and devious temptation—to rely on self and despair when self inevitably weakens or makes mistakes.

▶ **Lesson 4: Words can always hurt. Resist the temptation to say hurtful things when you're angry or tired.** Jesus warned against the temptation of evil speech. He taught that what makes a person defiled is what comes out of his mouth. This flew in the face of religious tradition at that time, which supposed that certain foods or eating habits could defile a person. Jesus rejected this concrete, superficial way of thinking about purity and defilement, pointing instead to what really defiles a person—the judgmental, ridiculing, or uncaring words that come *out* of his or her mouth. "But what comes out of the mouth proceeds from the heart, and this defiles a man. For out of the heart come evil thoughts, murder, adultery, fornication, theft, false witness, slander" (Matt. 15:18–19).

119

The old saying "Sticks and stones can break my bones, but words can never hurt me" is just not true, as we all have experienced. Words do cause great harm to their victims, even as they deteriorate the spirit of the person giving voice to them. Children can drive us crazy, and deep inside we're just children too. It's so hard to control ourselves when we're tired or overwhelmed with work and responsibilities. God knows that it's hard, but we must not defile ourselves by giving in to the temptation to say mean or rude things to our children, even when we're feeling stressed or ill.

Yet, as always, God stands ready to forgive if we slip up, which we've all done from time to time. The next time this happens to you, give yourself a time-out to ask God for forgiveness and to calm down. Then, as soon as you're up to it, apologize sincerely to your child for your reckless words. Your child will appreciate it more than you can imagine, and you can "undo" much if not all of the harm by taking this simple step.

▶ **Lesson 5: Beware of the temptation to follow those who seem righteous but aren't.** Jesus warned against following leaders or experts simply because they have prestige, power, or the appearance of respectability and righteousness. He cautioned people not to be taken in by correct-sounding or correct-looking individuals who can use the Scriptures to justify their own bad habits. He offered a guideline for discerning the true from the false. Look not at their power or degrees but at *their words and actions:*

> The hardest job kids face today is learning good manners without seeing any.
> Fred Astair

"Beware of false prophets, who come to you in sheep's clothing but inwardly are ravenous wolves. You will know them by their fruits. Are grapes gathered from thorns, or figs from thistles? So, every sound tree bears good fruit, but the bad tree bears evil fruit. A sound tree cannot bear evil fruit, nor can a bad tree bear

120

good fruit. Every tree that does not bear good fruit is cut down and thrown into the fire. Thus you will know them by their fruits."

Matthew 7:15–20

It's interesting that Jesus cautioned his followers to be aware of self-interest, even in religious leaders:

> And in his teaching he said, "Beware of the scribes, who like to go about in long robes, and to have salutations in the market places and the best seats in the synagogues and the places of honor at feasts, who devour widows' houses and for a pretense make long prayers. They will receive the greater condemnation."

Mark 12:38–40

When we're looking for guidance, it's easy to begin worshiping the experts, who seem to have it all together, claiming perfect judgment and righteousness, yet their words and manner often send a different message.

In a world of conflicting advice about parenting and spiritual growth, it's tempting simply to choose the person who looks or sounds righteous without looking deeper. Yet when we're looking for models to emulate as parents, we'd better be careful, for bad advice may work today but yield bad fruit many years from now. As happened with James, whose father used harsh discipline because he'd heard an expert say this was necessary to teach children to respect authority, the ill effects didn't show up until much later. The expert or neighbor who advises that we ignore our child's cries, feelings, or ideas or who urges us to be a strict disciplinarian poses a great danger not only to our child but to *us*, as Jesus pointedly warned: "Whoever receives one such child in my name receives me; but whoever causes one of these little ones who believe in me to sin, it would be better for him to have a great millstone fas-

> The teeth are smiling, but is the heart?
>
> Congo proverb

121

tened round his neck and to be drowned in the depth of the sea" (Matt. 18:5–6).

Children who grow distant, angry, or vengeful toward their parents are far more likely to sin, despite outward appearances of submission and obedience. Jesus wasn't fooled by appearances and said that the treasure of the heart would be seen in a person's words and actions. Accordingly, he warned that false prophets would preach in his name but end up leading people astray; that's why he asked his followers to evaluate leaders and experts by their fruit—their words and actions. Simply look and listen when the expert writes or speaks and compare what you see and hear with Jesus' charter. Nobody's perfect, but if you sense that there's a significant gap between the two, evaluate further before following that teacher. I saw a religious authority on a talk show recently whose "fruit" was rotten indeed. His loud, belligerent arguing, impatient interrupting, and condescending tone of voice silenced the other guests. Jesus said, "This people honors me with their lips, but their heart is far from me; in vain do they worship me, teaching as doctrines the precepts of men" (15:8–9).

Years from now, the experts won't be suffering because their instructions led our children down the wrong path—*we* will. We must use our own judgment when evaluating parenting advice, checking it against Jesus' charter to see if it fits. A good guideline is this: Those who guide us along the right path will ask us to follow *Jesus*, not *them*.

▶ **Lesson 6: Resist the temptation to pay more attention to money than to your child.** Jesus warned against the temptation to take on the values and trappings of materialism. Materialism leads to decreased compassion, increased greed, and paying more attention to money and things than our children and families.

And he said to them, "Take heed, and beware of all covetousness; for a man's life does not consist in the abundance of his possessions." And he told them a parable, saying, "The land of a rich man brought forth plentifully; and he thought to himself, 'What shall I do, for I have nowhere to store my crops?' And he said, 'I will do this: I will pull down my barns, and build larger ones; and there I will store all my grain and my goods. And I will say to my soul, Soul, you have ample goods laid up for many years; take your ease, eat, drink, be merry.' But God said to him, 'Fool! This night your soul is required of you; and the things you have prepared, whose will they be?' So is he who lays up treasure for himself, and is not rich toward God."

Luke 12:15–21

Magazine and television ads urge us to show we love our children by buying things for them. Are manufacturers saying that their products will make our children happy and spiritually grounded? According to Jesus, the best insurance for our children, despite all the slick commercials and glossy ads, is something you can't buy with cash or credit or debit cards. Purchased only with your lifelong effort and faith, this insurance consists of following, and making your child heir to, the principles of Jesus' charter. If you do this, despite all the mistakes, road bumps, and wrong turns that come with the territory of parenthood, you'll be building "a house on a rock," not a house on sand that will tumble when the first storms come. We can will to our children no greater fortune than this.

Most parents, if asked, would say they certainly value their children more than money or financial security. There's no doubt that they love them more than they love wealth. Yet remember, temptation is subtle and clever, slipping in under the door rather than knocking down the walls of our homes. Our priorities are only as good as the way we play them out through our behavior. If we objectively look at where we spend the most time, attention, and energy, we may discover that materialism has indeed crept into

> **Where your treasure is, there will your heart be also.**
>
> Jesus

123

our heart and mind, choking off what really matters most to us and to God.

Liz, a young corporate attorney, has a very hectic life and a very energetic preschooler named Megan. She came to me for counseling because she was torn. She had been told she would be made a partner within two years—almost unheard of at her age—if she was prepared to "do what it takes." Liz knew very well what that meant. "I've seen the way people work when they're trying to get that carrot being dangled in front of them. My friend Sam's a partner now, but I remember him working until ten or later most nights for years, and weekends too. And you know, I can't remember him smiling during that time or since! He's making a ton of money; he's made it. And I want to make it too. I want Megan to have everything she needs. I want her to have the best possible start in life. I want . . ."

Liz stopped midsentence and began fidgeting with the Palm Pilot she kept on her lap even during therapy sessions in case she remembered something she needed to do. Looking up, she began again, "I know, I know, this is that classic working-mother thing. But this time it's personal. I've got to give Eric an answer by Monday. I just want Megan to have the best possible start. . . ."

This is how temptation works. It doesn't walk up to your front door, ring the bell, and announce, "Hi, I'm Temptation, and I'm here to get you to focus on money and things and neglect the people you love." Instead, it whispers to you of your fondest dreams and dearest loves, "I'm just trying to help you do the right thing, so don't be selfish. You don't need all that time with your daughter. You say you want the best for her? Then don't be a wimp. Make the sacrifice now, and she'll have a great financial future tomorrow. Tell Eric you'll go for it. *Megan will be fine without you.*"

▶ **Lesson 7: Beware the temptations designed for your unique strengths and weaknesses.** Jesus knew temptation personally. His three temptations in the desert were not random but specific to Jesus' ministry. He was tempted to prove his divine source by making food out of stones, to use unrighteous means to achieve righteous ends, and to test his faith. Each time, he resisted the temptation not by arguing with or otherwise dwelling on Satan, the tempter, but by quoting Scripture and reminding himself of the right path, keeping his eyes on the prize.

Jesus' temptations were tailor-made for him, just as mine take advantage of my weaknesses, and yours seek out your Achilles' heel. I learned long ago by observing myself and others that temptation is not random, nor is it one-size-fits-all. Instead, it will always attach itself to our unique talents and aspirations. One of temptation's cleverest tricks is to seduce that which is a strength. Our strength can become our downfall because we're tripped up through the misuse or misdirection of our talents and ambitions. Liz's dilemma is a perfect example of this. Had she not been such a talented attorney, she'd never have been offered the career advancement that tempted her to work long hours, thus missing Megan's early years and weakening their mother-child connection.

Too Busy to Watch and Pray

Julie and Stan came to one parent group, but both said it would be tough to continue to attend due to their schedules. Clearly they were hoping for "the answer" that night and took notes as several parents spoke about helping their troubled children. More than once Julie said with some exasperation, "But Jen's never been this way before! She was always so good, so easy . . . I can't see why she's dropping out of school, constantly angry, and claiming to be depressed."

Other parents noted that many "good" kids go through hard times and have quite different feelings about themselves and about

125

life than they did when they were younger. I added that the anger, apathy, and sadness may be beyond the child's control.

Jen's parents seemed dissatisfied with this notion, pointing to the successes of their other three children and to Jen's high IQ, justifying their assumption that these problems must be intentional or just a passing phase. They never returned after that night. Their work continued to claim their time and attention.

Sadly, Jen deteriorated over the coming months. Her drug use increased, and she began living on the street or sleeping at her friends' homes. Somehow the connection she needed with her parents simply wasn't there.

What might have happened differently, I wondered, if Jen's parents had resisted the temptation to work harder so they wouldn't notice how serious Jen's problems had become and avoided the temptation to minimize and ignore what was really happening inside their child? Chances are, they could have seen Jen and found a way to meet their child's needs had they made a habit of Jesus' instruction to watch and pray.

For our own spiritual and personal development, we need to stay alert for signs that we are being pulled away from the higher road, the road that follows Jesus' teachings. I'll tell you a story that illustrates this, a story that is not lacking in irony.

While studying the Scriptures for this book, I've prayed daily, many times a day, to accurately communicate Jesus' teachings to my readers and to follow those teachings myself. One day my fourteen-year-old kept coming to my desk after school, asking me this and that, then saying several times, "Mama, come see what I learned in dance today!"

In exasperation I finally said, "Izzy, I *can't* come now. I've got to get this book written!" *Well, that's just great,* I thought. *I can't parent my child, even for a few minutes, because I'm too busy writing a book about parenting as Jesus would!* I said a quick prayer asking

> The only gift is a portion of thyself.
>
> Ralph Waldo Emerson

for forgiveness and shared an embarrassed laugh with God, then left my laptop to go watch a happy teenager perform her new steps for me.

With so many temptations from within and without, we may be overwhelmed. We can and should pray to avoid temptation whenever possible, because often it approaches us with some sort of lure, which may be disguised in a cloak of prestige, power, beauty, or sex appeal, or it may seem so reasonable—"Everybody's doing it." Of course, there are certain situations in which temptation is likely. A person who hates the taste of alcohol can go to a bar without being tempted, but this is not true for a recovering alcoholic. The only reliable self-defense is to maintain a realistic stance of prevention; that is, to recognize that temptations will come, whether directly or through the back door, and thus to watch for them, expect them, and resist them through prayer when they do come. Not only a spiritual leader but a wise psychologist as well, Jesus said as much: Watch and pray.

Remember and Reflect

When you were a child, what were the temptations you most wrestled with? They may have been overeating, explosive anger, not wanting to share, fighting, laziness, and so on. How well did you resist those temptations most of the time?

What do you think were your parents' primary temptations? Did they

> So many people feel that for humanity the game is up. Now no man can think like that and believe in God. If God is the God we believe him to be there is no room for pessimism. There may be remorse, regret; there may be penitence, contrition; there may be heart-searching, the realization of failure and of sin; but there can never be despair.
>
> William Barclay

127

include workaholism, gossiping, judgmentalism, anger, alcoholism, merciless behavior?

Do you see any connections between their temptations and those you experienced as a child? Can you see some similarities between your parents' temptations and those you're struggling against now?

What are the temptations that most often get in the way of maintaining a good relationship with your child, making good decisions, or pursuing your dreams?

How would you and your child benefit if you began to watch and pray to keep temptation away? What temptation, for you or your child, would Jesus urge you to watch for at this time?

PART 2

A New Paradigm for Guiding Your Child

"I am the good shepherd. The good shepherd lays down his life for the sheep. He who is a hireling and not a shepherd, whose own the sheep are not, sees the wolf coming and leaves the sheep and flees; and the wolf snatches them and scatters them. He flees because he is a hireling and cares nothing for the sheep. I am the good shepherd; I know my own and my own know me."

John 10:11–14

I've often said that we give baby showers when parents need them least, when they are holding an adorable newborn and receiving all kinds of attention. How about thirteen years later? *That's* when parents could really use a party! It really makes no sense that, as soon as the baby showers are over, we assume that we're on our own and shouldn't need help from other parents. Yet this is exactly when our challenges begin. Once all the attention has waned, we find ourselves looking at a baby for whom we will be responsible our whole lives.

129

I remember sitting in our mobile home, looking at my infant with the sudden realization that my carefree adolescence was over: *Oh my goodness, I'll be responsible for her for the next eighteen years!* I was shocked, even frightened. I'd owned two cats, but this was altogether different. Ah, the thoughts that run through a twenty-year-old's mind!

How very naïve I was. When my daughter turned eighteen, my responsibility certainly did not end. In fact, I entered a brand new, extremely important phase of parenting, the one that lasts as long as a parent lives—parenting the adult child. This requires a delicate balance between respectful guidance and friendship.

My need for Jesus' teachings and example only grew as the years went by, and they never failed to guide me—when I remembered to consult them. Like anyone else, I sometimes got caught up in my own feelings and needs, such that I couldn't see my daughter's needs. At such times, it's easy to forget that we have a blueprint, we have a model, we have a guide.

Guidance and Shepherding versus Training and Discipline

As parents, we are responsible for guiding our children. This is a wiser, deeper, and more encompassing goal than simply disciplining or training. To accomplish this task, we need a guide. In Jesus' charter and in our relationship with God, that guide is ours, always available. Jesus was aware that the way he guided his disciples was pivotal, for it led not only to their (gradually) becoming more self-disciplined and spiritually mature but to an abiding trust in him.

> The thing about having a baby is that thereafter you have it.
>
> Jean Kerr

"Truly, truly, I say to you, he who does not enter the sheepfold by the door but climbs in by another way, that man is a thief and a rob-

130

ber; but he who enters by the door is the shepherd of the sheep. To him the gatekeeper opens; the sheep hear his voice, and he calls his own sheep by name and leads them out. When he has brought out all his own, he goes before them, and the sheep follow him, for they know his voice. A stranger they will not follow, but they will flee from him, for they do not know the voice of strangers."

John 10:1–5

You'll be amazed at the insights that will come to you, while sorting out a vexing problem with your child, when you simply ask yourself or a friend, "How would Jesus raise my child in this situation?" There are many benefits for the child whose parent regularly asks this question. Take a look at some of the benefits you'll be giving your child as you embark on this journey.

Effects on Your Child

With the world's approach to raising children, children tend to:	With Jesus' approach to raising children, children tend to:
be competitive with others, even when unnecessary	be competitive or cooperative, depending on the situation
be self-confident when winning, not when losing—confidence based on performance and praise	be self-confident when trying their best—confidence based on effort and commitment
be obedient when monitored; need ongoing discipline, relying on others to control behavior	be cooperative whether or not someone is watching; need guidance while developing self-control
grow increasingly rebellious and/or distant as they get older	grow increasingly close to parent and mature as they get older
be materialistic/money focused	make spirituality, family, and friends highest priorities
be spiritually cynical, apathetic, or hypocritical	be earnest in spiritual seeking, even if they experience doubts
follow the crowd	follow inner values/goals
try to get their way, not noticing how it affects you	pursue their goals, but empathize with your feelings

131

Children adopt their parents' emotional styles, coping strategies, and habits—both good and bad. We must, in the course of raising them, teach them how to determine what's right and what's wrong, how to handle conflict, how to set and achieve goals, and how to accomplish all the little daily tasks that most adults take for granted (brushing teeth, cleaning one's room, caring for pets, studying for exams, and so on).

Jesus understood that those under his care would tend to follow his example. Likewise, for good or for ill, our children are likely to become a lot like us: "He also told them a parable: 'Can a blind man lead a blind man? Will they not both fall into a pit? A disciple is not above his teacher, but every one when he is fully taught will be like his teacher'" (Luke 6:39–40).

Consider the example of a child, when fully taught, turning out to be like his parent. A young person takes a strong political position that is the opposite of his parent's, and frequent loud arguments and hurt feelings ensue over the years. Some people are fooled by this situation, thinking that in this case the child certainly hasn't turned out to be like his parent. Not so. The parent's unintended influence on the child has indeed been successful. Parent and child are now *identical* in their habitual certainty, all-or-none thinking, and poor control over a hot temper. Only the contents of the political beliefs—which are, ironically, far less potent in terms of their effects on relationships and lives—differ. The child (who would hate to hear this) *has indeed become like the teacher*—in this case the parent whose ideas he so abhors. The sad, angry parent will spend a lifetime wondering what went wrong, why his child doesn't "know his voice"—identify with the parent—instead preferring the company of others.

Jesus guided—shepherded—his disciples, who could indeed wander off into worldly thinking and behavior without his monitoring and direction, particularly when they first began working together. Jesus wanted to guide them away from destructive patterns and toward positive ways of relating to God and other people, but he didn't want them to fear him. When a child fears his or her parent, in a sense the child no longer knows the parent's voice.

Like many therapists, I've worked with countless people who don't see their parents as friends, and no longer respond to their parents' words. This is especially unfortunate when their parents have grown or matured and now have some good advice to offer! But something in the relationship snapped long ago; some trust was broken. Yet despite what some pessimistic experts say, many of these breakages *can* be repaired if the parents are willing to pray for help—as Jesus said, things that are impossible with people are possible with God—but parents must commit themselves to making the first move.

It's become commonplace to see headlines telling us how to train or discipline our children, but I worry about the effects that such words have on us as parents. They suggest that our children are passive and, like rats in behavioral research, learn by being manipulated and subjected to a program of rewards and punishments. The result is that parents end up feeling more like the Pavlovian scientist in his starched white coat than thoughtful human beings. This emphasis on forcing rather than shepherding can lead us, and our children, astray.

One day when I was eleven and my brother was two, he wouldn't stop throwing sand at other toddlers, so I felt I should discipline him. I threw sand at him in the same way, saying, "See how it feels when you do that?" What I *didn't* know was that the sand would get deep into his eyes, causing him great pain, and that he would look at me with hurt and distrust long after I, weeping with regret, washed it out. I could have helped him learn the same lesson, without my modeling poor behavior, by letting him know that he would have to leave the park if he threw more sand, then carrying through with the consequences if he disobeyed. If only I had known how, I would have taught him wisely instead of "disciplining" him foolishly.

Indeed, when it comes to guiding a child, ignorance is not bliss. *If only* is a phrase that countless parents have used: "If only we'd known." But just as Jesus didn't expect his disciples to know already how to guide others, we are not expected to know already how to raise our child as Jesus would. It's a long-term learning process, requiring a lot of prayer, trial-and-error experimentation, patience, and faith.

A Tale of Guidance and Shepherding

On a hot summer day, I watched a sixteen-year-old boy "shepherding" his young cousins as they played together in a hotel pool. Imagine this real-life scene, and you may be able to discern the kind of shepherding approach that Jesus used to "raise" and guide his disciples. While throwing the laughing third graders into the water, the young man suddenly stopped playing and looked in horror at the children. I wondered what had upset him and noticed that the children were making a game of taking water in their mouths and then spitting it out. The older boy stiffened and adopted a professorial tone: "Don't spit in the pool!" They asked why, and he answered, "Because it's nasty, and—you did it again!" he said in disbelief.

The siblings looked at each other, then at him. "What's wrong with it?" the girl asked. Their cousin held himself upright again in water to his waist, explaining in slow, formal tones: "This is a hotel. People come from all over the country and swim in this pool, and *you are drinking that in.*"

The young boy responded, "Well, I spit it out, so it's okay."

The sixteen-year-old said, "Oh, great! That's like saying somebody stabbed you with a knife, but it's okay because they pulled it out!"

The children, looking right at their impromptu teacher, spit water at each other and giggled.

The adults sitting by the pool, including me, sat with bemused tension, waiting to see how he would respond to this defiance. He simply swam away, making it clear that he wouldn't be playing with such unhygienic people.

I glanced at the defiant brother and sister, cheeks full of pool water. They spat it out joylessly, this time eyeing it with suspicion, then swam toward their cousin. He received them in the style of a father accepting his rebellious prodigal son and played with them again.

Let's look at the process. First, the older and wiser cousin had been playing with the children for hours, spending time with them, and through this symbolic conduct, showing his approval and liking of them. But being children with minds and wills of their own, they'd tested him when he gave them an instruction.

Next, he responded not by yelling louder but by teaching them directly. This didn't work, *so he changed tactics*, telling them a parable they could understand. But even this didn't work, so he swam away and refused to play with them. Finally, the children began to wonder what might be in that water they were holding in their mouths. Then they swam back to their offended cousin, asking for another chance, which he gave them.

We observers could see that they'd gotten the point but hadn't wanted to lose face by admitting that they'd been doing something quite foolish. As often happens, their cousin's teaching didn't yield fruit in the short-term but will certainly do so in the long-term.

Despite all appearances of his words falling on stony ground, the young man's efforts were not in vain. The children did learn; if their sickly expressions when they last spit out the water were any indication, they will never do that again. But they would not have seriously considered what he had to teach them were he not someone they adored and wanted to spend time with. Had he not been making deposits in their emotional bank account, he could not have had lasting influence on them. Had his spirit been angry, disgusted, or impatient, he would have had, at best, momentary control over them. The adults around the pool looked at one another, smiled, and were tempted to break into applause for some splendid shepherding indeed.

6

Spiritual Guidance

"Let the little children come to me."
Mark 10:14

Children form impressions of God based on what they observe in and experience with their parents. For good or for bad, children tend to view God as they see their parents, including their habits, attitudes, even hair color! Through our words and symbolic conduct, we send the message that God is a harsh judge, who is always looking for reasons to criticize, correct, and punish, or that he is a loving parent who is always looking for opportunities to listen, forgive, and guide.

Take a moment to imagine the scene. Lots of people are crowded together, straining to get closer to hear Jesus. See the disciples trying their best to maintain some crowd control. The children, brought long distances by tired but hopeful parents, are noisy and distracting. This is their one chance, their one shot at getting their child near the man they'd heard about, this Jesus of Nazareth who cared for the poor, the sick, and even the sinners. They want him to see their children, perhaps to heal them physically or mentally, and above all to bless them. But the disciples begin to shoo them away; after all, these are only children. Surely Jesus didn't have time for this silliness; children can't understand his teachings, so why bother him with this intrusion?

If you've heard this story before, it was probably presented as a sweet story illustrating Jesus' love for little children. We picture a pleasant scene with a calm, smiling Jesus surrounded by calm, smiling children. Occasionally the story is used in religious services to highlight our relationship with God, who never turns us away (more on this in a moment). Only rarely, however, is the point made that these were wiggling, messy, noisy, real-life children in whose defense Jesus was reprimanding his disciples. On many occasions, Jesus' symbolic conduct conveyed the importance he placed on children and parents. His words went even further, asserting that children exemplify the spirit required for anyone who wishes to enter the kingdom of God.

Learning from Jesus

Jesus taught in many ways that, in God's eyes, *children and adults are equally important and valuable.* Our child's spiritual development is as important to God as our own. Hence it is our duty to make sure that our children feel free to come to us and to God. We don't want our children to turn away from religion, dismiss it as hypocrisy, or become legalistic and hypocritical. Parents, committed to raising their children as Jesus would, will do everything in their power to provide an environment that supports a positive view of God and genuine spiritual growth.

▶ **Lesson 1: Let your child come to God.**

> And they were bringing children to him, that he might touch them; and the disciples rebuked them. But when Jesus saw it he was indignant, and said to them, "Let the children come to me,

do not hinder them; for to such belongs the kingdom of God. Truly, I say to you, whoever does not receive the kingdom of God like a child shall not enter it." And he took them in his arms and blessed them, laying his hands upon them.

Mark 10:13–16

Jesus was not happy with the disciples' attempt to shoo the children away. In fact, he was indignant! This strong word reveals much about Jesus' view of children and their importance to God. He not only told his disciples to let the children come to him; he went so far as to uphold children as the *model* for any adult who wants to enter the kingdom of God. Jesus was sending the message that we must not do anything, even if well-intentioned, that could keep a child away from God.

You may feel that you have already let your children come to God by taking them to worship services or religious education classes. It's great if you're already doing this; if not, you can get them started in such activities at any time. Yet there are other important ways of letting children come to God. One way is spiritual; we must make sure that we depict the kind of God a child can approach with confidence. Another way is psychological; we create, through our words and behavior, conditions that are favorable for a trusting relationship with God.

A key influence on a child's spiritual development is what he or she learns and experiences in worship services. While most religious communities no longer expect small children to sit for an hour or longer in silent attention to adult language that is, for the most part, over their heads, some churches subtly pressure parents to force their children to do so. We don't force adults to attend services conducted in a language they don't understand, nor would we dream of preventing an elderly person from leaving early if he or she can't sit comfortably throughout the service. How can we show less concern for a child's capacity to understand or for his or her physical limitations?

139

The spirit of Jesus' command to "let the children come to me" is violated when their spiritual development is disregarded. While the minister or priest is speaking of a loving, merciful God, a restless child is yanked back onto the pew or dragged outside to be spanked. While the choir is singing "What a friend we have in Jesus," a parent pulls her child close, whispering in his ear not the words to the song but a physical threat. I think it's time we asked ourselves exactly what these children are learning.

What view of God will children have when worship services are juxtaposed with unrealistic expectations, rigid control, and violence? One woman, remembering the Sunday threats and spankings she'd endured from her father, had assumed—as had her father and a great many people—that the King James translation of the verse "Suffer the little children to come unto me" means that children have to *suffer* to come to Jesus. How antithetical to all that Jesus stood for! How he would have cringed or wept!

We can be thankful that many congregations now offer a separate children's service during the adult service. This is wise and a blessing for energetic children, who can be taught about God in an age-appropriate setting, *and* for parents, who would dearly love to be able to sit in peace and actually hear the sermon or homily. Parents, especially those with young children, *need* this time with God to recharge their spiritual batteries so that they can better model Jesus' teachings. Those congregations that provide for these needs are helping both the child and the parent come to God.

Parents and children alike will benefit when a culture of control is replaced with a culture of worship. Some congregations print a statement in their weekly bulletin saying that

> There are two kinds of morality side by side: one which we preach but do not practice, and the other which we practice but seldom preach.
>
> Bertrand Russell

140

babies and children are highly valued and that parents should take advantage of nurseries or other help when their children cry or otherwise make it difficult for people around them to hear. When there is no formal child care available, parents, especially those who are striving to raise their children as Jesus would, can post an invitation for all parents to meet and discuss options to meet the spiritual needs of both parents and children during services. These could include co-op babysitting and classes for young children or pooling money to hire child care providers. If all else fails, parents can take quiet activities for their children to do during the service or they can walk them outside when they become restless. Some parents have sought new places to worship simply because of a lack of competent child care. What a shame!

▶ **Lesson 2: If you make the soil good, Jesus' teachings will take root and grow.** Jesus taught that spiritual development occurs when the seed of his teaching falls on fertile, protected ground:

> And he told them many things in parables, saying: "A sower went out to sow. And as he sowed, some seeds fell along the path, and the birds came and devoured them. Other seeds fell on rocky ground, where they had not much soil, and immediately they sprang up, since they had no depth of soil, but when the sun rose they were scorched; and since they had no root they withered away. Other seeds fell upon thorns, and the thorns grew up and choked them. Other seeds fell on good soil and brought forth grain, some a hundredfold, some sixty, some thirty."
>
> Matthew 13:3–8

We as parents can help our children grow spiritually by preparing their spiritual soil. Depending on the way we treat our children and represent God to them, they will grow up to be able and eager to receive Jesus' teachings and God's Spirit or unable and unwilling to do so.

141

Jesus taught and modeled a patient, long-term approach to spiritual instruction and guidance. He told his disciples to teach others about God while having faith, simplicity, and generosity; never taking advantage of others or being opportunistic; not being a burden; and never arguing or demanding. They were to do their best to communicate Jesus' message, then accept the results, whatever they were. When Jesus taught, he never expected instant results. He knew that for a seed to grow, it needs time and the right conditions.

Does this sound easy? Maybe it does at first blush—just be laid back, teach and model Jesus' teachings, and don't worry about your child's response. But, oh, how difficult it is to carry out! Your child's spiritual and character development matters a great deal to you, or you wouldn't be reading this book. How then are you to be laid back when your child seems disinterested or even cynical? It's a discouraging feeling to tell a good parable of your own or make an important point, only to have your child respond with a bored "uh-huh" and run off to play or watch TV. Did anything sink in? Are you just talking to yourself? Is it even worth trying to teach that child anything of a spiritual or moral nature?

Your teaching *will* take root if the conditions are right; if you deliver it with faith, simplicity, and generosity; if you don't take advantage of your authority over your children; if you don't burden them with unrealistic expectations; and if you avoid arguing and making unreasonable demands. But don't count on seeing results right away. In fact, your child is *least* likely to signal that they got it when they *most* need what you're trying to teach them. When their minds and hearts are troubled, they can't very well say, "Thank you for instilling in me this valuable lesson. I will apply it to my life at once." Expect instead something on the order of a pivotal encounter in the movie *Sister Act 2*, in which a heartseeing teacher tried to reach a hostile, mixed-up student.

Teacher: (Whoopi Goldberg): Listen, you have just a little bit more attitude than I like, but I've decided I'm gonna *dog* you no matter what.

Student: (Lauryn Hill), rolling her eyes: Okay, I'm listening to you. Go ahead.

Teacher: I know you want to sing. I love to sing. Nothing makes me happier. I either wanted to be a singer or the head of the Ice Capades.

(Student rolls her eyes.)

Teacher: Hey, you know what the Ice Capades are? Don't roll your eyes. They were very cool. [She then tells a story about an author advising young writers.] I'm gonna say the same thing to you. If you wake up in the morning and you can't think of anything but singing first, then you're supposed to be a singer, girl.

Student, looking annoyed: What's the point of your story, Sister? What's the point?

Teacher: Read the book [gives her the book]. And don't roll your eyes about the Ice Capades. It was a very good living. I just want to point that out.

(Student walks away.)

This teacher had faith. She knew that children *most* need help when they're *least* likely to admit it or show signs of having received it. She knew that her student needed time in which to process the little parable she'd told about following one's dreams. The teacher *had* gotten through that tough exterior by telling a short, interesting story, without lecturing and with a great deal of empathy. Her heartseeing ability allowed her to see the girl's discouraged spirit and broken dreams, which in turn allowed her to plant a seed that would blossom and grow.

Jesus' story about the four types of soil helped prepare the disciples for the tough job of teaching ahead of them. As they spread the Good News, their reception would not always be warm. Often they would feel as though nothing they said was sinking in or making a difference. Some people would not want to hear anything they had to say. Others would listen but wouldn't get it, and still others would understand, then seem to promptly forget what they had heard. Jesus reassured his disciples that when the seed of his teachings fell in fertile conditions, it would grow beautifully.

Nobody can mandate spiritual growth. We aren't God. We're just parents who care. For those who dare to strive toward parenting as Jesus would, helping children grow spiritually is more like being a gardener than a professor. The goal is to *prepare the soil* in which Jesus' teachings can take root and grow. How can we do this? William Barclay analyzes what Jesus said: "The good ground was deep and clean and soft; the seed could gain an entry; it could find nourishment; it could grow unchecked; and in the good ground it brought forth an abundant harvest."[1] This parable provides parents with an excellent "gardening" plan:

Conditions of the good soil	Conditions of good spiritual soil	How parents can make the soil good
The soil was deep, clean, and soft.	The child's spirit is open, not hardened by fear, anger, self-loathing, or loneliness.	Parents make an effort to *see and hear* their child. They guide and teach rather than control and discipline.
The seed could get deep into the ground.	The child's spirit isn't on guard or defensive due to being blamed, criticized, or guilt-tripped. The child is trusting and open with adults.	When the child behaves in a poor or immature way, parents seek to understand why, then redirect to a better way. They never use blame or guilt.
The seed could find nourishment.	Active listening and fellowship help Jesus' teachings take root.	Parents listen patiently without interrupting. They help their child find peers who are open to God.
The seed could grow without interference.	There is adequate exposure to Jesus' teachings, which helps the child internalize them. Children do not witness adult hypocrisy.	Parents teach gently, only in teachable moments, not too much or too often. They are able to give the child room and freedom to grow. *They practice what they preach.*

As you can see, none of the things that parents can do to make the soil good can be done all at once. They require time and patience. As a Chinese proverb says, "We don't have enough time to hurry." You can't force a seed to grow any faster. As I have learned from many a failed gardening project, fiddling with the seed or adding too much fertilizer and water causes the seedling to wither. All that concern was not good for it. Parents must do their best and let God do the rest.

You may know the story of the bamboo plant. It must receive nutrients and water for six years while it hibernates in the ground. Only in the sixth year does it grow visibly—but when it does, it reaches five feet or more in just a few months! So it is with Jesus' teachings. We may not see the fruit of them in our child for several years. This means that we must persevere in being there for our children, trusting that our gentle and loving attitude toward them is having an effect, whether or not we see visible results.

Alan Nelson notes that abiding—simply *being with* God and sticking to our plan—is a better goal than trying to force growth on our timetable.

> God is primarily process-oriented, not product-oriented. In John 15, Jesus tells us to abide in him in order to bear fruit. It is the abiding that is the process. . . . Our natural inclination is to focus on the fruit bearing. We read books, go to seminars, and listen to cassettes on better fruit bearing. What we need to think about is better abiding. When we improve the process, the fruit will come naturally.[2]

▶ **Lesson 3: Avoid "false advertising"—to your child, God is just like you.** Parents can make or break a child's desire to know God. We can prepare in him or her good soil or fashion a future cynic, hypocrite, or legalistic person with little compassion for others. As I've told some of my patients

> Children need love, especially when they do not deserve it.
>
> Harold Hulbert

145

who were raised with harsh punishments or endless criticism, "Your view of God as harsh and critical is a product of your parent's inadvertent 'false advertising'!" The problem isn't just the way these people were treated as children. It is also their parents' blindness to their true feelings and needs. For a parent to treat a child in a harsh way, the parent must be, or force himself or herself to be, heartblind—unseeing and uncaring about the child's feelings. Otherwise, the parent couldn't behave that way. Not only is it painful and alienating to a child when he or she feels unseen in this way, but the added danger is that the child may assume that God is likewise unable to see, hence unable to care about, his or her real self or true feelings.

When Jesus responded to and healed the woman who touched the hem of his garment, he demonstrated that God perceives even our slightest need. Before she said a word, he felt her touch and *sensed* her feelings and her need. Not afflicted with the world's hectic self-focus, he could see with his heart:

> And there was a woman who had had a flow of blood for twelve years, and who had suffered much under many physicians, and had spent all that she had, and was no better but rather grew worse. She had heard the reports about Jesus, and came up behind him in the crowd and touched his garment. For she said, "If I touch even his garments, I shall be made well." And immediately the hemorrhage ceased; and she felt in her body that she was healed of her disease. And Jesus, perceiving in himself that power had gone forth from him, immediately turned about in the crowd, and said, "Who touched my garments?" And his disciples said to him, "You see the crowd pressing around you, and yet you say, 'Who touched me?'" And he looked around to see who had done it. But the woman, knowing what had been done to her, came in fear and trembling and fell down before him, and told him the whole truth. And he said to her, "Daughter, your faith has made you well; go in peace, and be healed of your disease."
>
> Mark 5:25–34

146

Jesus not only demonstrated his sensitivity to others' needs by his response to those who came to him for healing, he also made the point over and over again that we are "blind" until we ask God to help us see more clearly. Repeatedly in the Gospels, Jesus restores vision to the blind, which is symbolic of our need for God's healing of our own heartblindness. Only when this is healed can we truly see others, including our child:

> And they came to Bethsaida. And some people brought to him a blind man, and begged him to touch him. And he took the blind man by the hand, and led him out of the village; and when he had spit on his eyes and laid his hands upon him, he asked him, "Do you see anything?" And he looked up and said, "I see men; but they look like trees, walking." Then again he laid his hands upon his eyes; and he looked intently and was restored, and saw everything clearly.
>
> Mark 8:22–25

While waiting for my daughter at the orthodontist's office, I heard a toddler crying pitifully from another room. A sharp "Don't know, don't care!" was her mother's only response to every whimper. Those of us sitting nearby glanced uncomfortably at one another. We've all been there, either frustrated to the point of screaming or crying or witnessing someone else at that breaking point. Children, especially babies and toddlers, exact a toll on one's nervous system that only a parent can understand. It's hard to keep a level head when surrounded by constant whining, colicky screaming, or ear-splitting tantrums. Who could blame us for getting frazzled under such conditions? Jesus taught that God knows our limitations and that we are all tempted to behave in ways that don't reflect our highest values.

But the sad toddler doesn't know any of this. All she knows is that her mom doesn't know and doesn't care. Eventually, when she finds someone else to reach out to, she'll stop crying

147

to her mother. As she learns to stifle her feelings, she'll start acting them out in rage attacks, drug use, or early sex, or by running away or becoming depressed and filled with self-loathing.

This mother was quite right. She *didn't* know what her child was feeling, because she couldn't see her with her heart; thus she couldn't imagine the physical sensations, thoughts, and emotions that were causing her child to cry. And because she couldn't imagine the various reasons that could account for the crying, she had neither the desire nor the ability to discover the cause and respond to it. Not being able to imagine another person's feelings is a serious matter, especially for parents, because lack of imagination limits the possibility of identifying the causes for our child's feelings. Parents like the mother at the doctor's office are angry much of the time, but not because they don't love their children. Their anger flows from their own untended wounds and bottled-up feelings. Worsening the hole in their spirit is a sense of failure, having learned that nothing they do seems to comfort their child.

This mother probably tells herself that she's tried everything, so it must be the child's fault that she's fussy. *She's just a fussy baby, maybe spoiled too. So don't worry about crying spells: "Don't know; don't care."* You've surely seen such parents in stores, pushing their children in strollers or shopping carts in a state of oblivion; they seem not to hear the crying, pleading, or screaming of which everyone else is keenly aware. For them, a child's cries are no more meaningful than the squeak of a rusty hinge.

Though they may rationalize their indifference to their children's distress as some kind of discipline that will keep them from being spoiled, the reality is that they can *never really know* why their children say what they say, do what they do, or feel what

> Children have never been very good at listening to their elders, but they have never failed to imitate them.
>
> James Baldwin

they feel. The cries of anger, need, fear, loneliness, or pain thus seem totally unjustified, random, mean-spirited, or out of the blue. Naturally, this leads them to respond in ways that are woefully inadequate and that erode the child's sense of trust.

Because children see God as they see their parents, children raised by heartblind parents won't expect God to accept them or understand their feelings. It amazes me to hear experts actually *advise* us (and this is what many weary parents want to hear) simply to ignore our children's cries, telling us to let our children "cry it out" instead. We should ask, *What is it, precisely, that our children are supposed to be crying out?* The hope that someone will help them? That someone will care?

Parents who want to raise their child as Jesus would must ask the hard questions and refuse to accept pat answers, because experts are naturally focused on helping us get some sleep or stop worrying or solve whatever problem we're having *right now* in the short-term. The experts won't have to live with the long-term results of their advice; *we* will. And most important, our child will. Over time, as children continue to cry out with no response from their parents, they lose their ability to trust. They abandon all hope that adults will care about and respond to their needs for reassurance and comforting or even for food and drink.

I remember a landlord's daughter who brought her baby to the rental office, which was next to our apartment. Hour after hour, day after day, the infant cried. I played with him whenever I could and appealed to the young mother to respond to his vigorous cries. But she could not be moved; she'd read in a book, "If you don't let them cry it out, they'll be spoiled." Over the coming months, the baby became increasingly docile, quiet, and listless. By the time we moved, he was no longer tracking objects with his eyes, playing with his fingers, or even bothering to look up when someone entered the room. He'd certainly cried it out. What's the point of crying for help or looking to adults for comfort if that help and comfort are never given?

Children raised by such parents will view God as likewise unresponsive to their distress, a judge or a boss to whom they would never come when confused or weary. "Don't know; don't care."

Counseling helps those who see and admit they need help. But what about the rest? How likely are they to enter counseling when, like this mother, they don't see any problem with their behavior because they read it in a book or because this is how their parents raised them?

Those who commit themselves to parenting as Jesus would have the great advantage of being able to compare their behaviors with his teachings constantly. This can alert them to dangerous gaps and spur loving but wounded parents to seek the help and support they need. We must be sure to reach out to such parents whenever we can, or they and their children may never trust God *or* other people to care about them or to guide and support them when they need help.

Think back to some time when trouble or tragedy hit you. There was someone you wanted to go to. Who was this person? What did you want from him or her? Chances are, you simply wanted to be in the person's presence, to know he or she understood what you were going through. Now you're getting closer to the deeper meaning of Jesus' words, "Let the children come to me." If you've ever said to someone going through a frightening or sad time, "Remember, you can always come to me," or "Call me if you need to talk," then you've behaved as Jesus did when he let the children come to him. You've made it easy for the person to come to you, to *really* come to you, with his or her heart's needs. We must

> To teach a child to love God and have Jesus as a friend and a role model in the way He treated people is to give a child a wholly different approach to morality. The child will still value the Commandments, but will now aspire to ideals far beyond the mere minimal requirements of the Commandments.
>
> Joseph Girzone

150

do this for our children so that they feel free—not reluctant, afraid, or unable—to come to us. Most important, we want them to feel that they can also come to God.

Now more than ever, we must be there for our children. We can't afford to rely on the world's values, such as materialism, vindictiveness, selfishness, and cynicism, when raising them.

Recently, as I was walking downtown, I saw on the sidewalk a panting baby bird, its leg and wing broken and clearly near death. I felt a terrible sadness. The suffering bird made me think about the thirteen-year-old boy who, earlier this year, shot another boy to death at my daughter's school over some silly thing—two futures ruined, two families grieving. What happened to this boy's spirit in his short time on earth? What might have been different had the seed of Jesus' teachings been planted, taken root, and grown in his spirit long ago?

The bird appeared to have been pushed out of the nest too early. It was barely moving now; the end was near. I rubbed its back gently, hoping to ease its sense of total abandonment and lonely suffering. It startled at first, but then closed its eyes in rest. I thought, *We really mustn't waste a moment.*

As Jesus said, "The harvest is plentiful but the workers are few" (Matt. 9:37 NIV). Everyone needs to work together to do all we can to repair a wounded generation of children. *Every single person* who has received the call to raise children as Jesus would and has answered yes is desperately needed—not only by his or her own children but by *all* children. We must model for them a God who cares and will respond to their distress, a God to whom they can come when overwhelmed with rage and confusion.

Our responsibility to encourage children to come to Jesus can be fulfilled only when we make certain that we have helped them become the good soil in which his teachings can take root. This can challenge our commitment,

> One of the great spiritual laws is that one comes to resemble what one worships.
>
> N. T. Wright

151

wisdom, and strength, especially when sometimes we don't feel like good soil ourselves. What happens when we are feeling lost, perhaps abandoned by God? How can we then help our children lean toward God in those difficult moments? The answer lies in the word *commitment*. Our commitment is more resilient and reliable than our motivation, willpower, or enthusiasm. Commitment says: I may be having my doubts about God; I may be angry at God during this trying time in my life; my burdens may be too heavy for me, yet I will continue to gently soften, water, and fertilize the soil of my child's spirit. Maybe my efforts at this time will be small or insignificant, but I will continue to nurture that soil however I can, because that is all that is expected of me. As Mother Teresa said, "God doesn't require us to succeed; he only requires that we try."

Remember and Reflect

How often did you feel really seen and cared about when you were a child? How might things have been different then and now if Jesus had raised you?

Were your own parents seen as they were growing up, or did they inherit heartblindness?

How did your parents' ability (or inability) to see your needs and feelings affect your self-esteem, confidence, and ability to read other people's feelings? What effect did this have on you as a child? What effects do you still experience now?

What memories do you have of religious training? Were you exposed to Jesus' teachings? Did your parents practice what they preached? What about their parents?

What image of God did you have as a child—loving, trusting, judgmental, critical? Is that image still with you today? Does it need repair or a complete overhaul?

How could Jesus help you improve your heartseeing ability? What would Jesus say is your child's greatest spiritual need right now?

7

Encouraging Your Child's Potential

"Every one to whom much is given, of him will much be required."

Luke 12:48

In following Jesus' methods for helping others reach their potential, you may have to take on some new responsibilities. At the same time, you'll feel released from the cultural expectation that parents can, with sufficient determination, bestow talents and competencies on their children. This unrealistic notion leads to much unhappiness and prevents the discovery of a child's natural talents. If Jesus' methods brought out such amazing gifts in his adult followers, imagine what they can do for your still-developing child.

If you believe what you see on TV and film, a child simply takes lessons, becomes a virtuoso, then performs in Carnegie Hall or wins the Nobel prize. All his or her parents need do is watch and applaud. What a happy ending! It's easy to buy into the idea that gifted children faithfully develop their skills in an area approved by their parents, are consistently motivated, never fail to practice or complete homework, and

155

never, ever fail. As parents, we want our beloved children to do their best, but if we're expecting their progress to be smooth and without misstep, we (and they) are in for difficult times ahead.

How can we help our child live up to his or her potential? Our responsibility is not to create a prodigy but to provide our child with prodigious quantities of guidance, encouragement, and patience. Whatever our child's strengths and limitations, we can do as Jesus did with his disciples—become sensitive to our child's interests or potential interests and help our child fully invest and develop his or her talents.

Learning from Jesus

Jesus valued each of the disciples personally and did all he could to provide a supportive environment in which their strengths could blossom. Particularly in light of the fact that he had no college campus, training center, or facilities of any kind to offer, his development of the disciples' talents was truly impressive. The learning environment he created for them was psychological and spiritual, consisting of his careful "raising" of them. This environment is something that every parent can afford, because it is free to all those who commit themselves to learning and practicing the methods Jesus used to help his disciples become all they could be.

▶ **Lesson 1: Match your expectations to your child's abilities.** Jesus revealed a God who is fair. He is a God who knows we don't all have the same number, quality, or type of gifts. In democratic societies, it's easy to get lulled into believing that we're all equal. Well, perhaps we're relatively equal under the law, but we're certainly not equal in our strengths or talents. Jesus told this parable to illustrate God's sliding scale of requirements, calibrated according to our strength and ability:

156

The Lord said, "Who then is the faithful and wise steward, whom his master will set over his household, to give them their portion of food at the proper time? Blessed is that servant whom his master when he comes will find so doing. Truly I tell you, he will set him over all his possessions. But if that servant says to himself, 'My master is delayed in coming,' and begins to beat the menservants and the maidservants, and to eat and drink and get drunk, the master of that servant will come on a day when he does not expect him and at an hour he does not know, and will punish him, and put him with the unfaithful. And that servant who knew his master's will, but did not make ready or act according to his will, shall receive a severe beating. But he who did not know, and did what deserved a beating, shall receive a light beating. Every one to whom much is given, of him will much be required; and of him to whom men commit much they will demand the more."

Luke 12:42–48

In Jesus' day, slavery and corporal punishment went hand in hand. He certainly didn't tell this parable to condone either; they were common in that society and, as usual, he taught using images that were familiar to his listeners. One point that he was making here is that we should not slack off when nobody's watching. In this case, he was speaking metaphorically of those who behave badly and think they can get away with it because the master (representing Jesus or, more generally, God[1]) is away.

The second lesson he's trying to convey is that God expects more of those to whom more has been given—and less of those to whom less is given. This is an ultimate fairness. If your child is gifted, God will expect more of him or her. If your child has learning problems or a psychological disorder, you can be thankful that God will expect less. (This goes for parents too. It's reassuring to know we're not expected to pressure ourselves unrealistically to do more or be more than we're able, though we must do our very best with what we have.) We need not try

157

to create gifts that aren't there; we have only to develop those that are.

While working with children with Down's syndrome, I found that their lives differed drastically not in terms of their native abilities but in the degree to which those abilities were developed. And this had everything to do with their parents' attitudes and expectations. I remember one family in which the parents seemed sad, and they felt very sorry for their only child, Robbie, fearing he'd never be happy. They were kind people, and I could understand their feelings. Then I began working with another family, in which Peter, the child with Down's, was the youngest. The house was a whirlwind, his four siblings in constant motion. Peter's parents were thus very busy and insisted that Peter learn to do many things on his own. The difference was really remarkable. Here was a boy whose language and other skills weren't that different from Robbie's during testing but whose feelings of confidence and acceptance as "just one more kid in the family" gave his life an altogether different flavor. His parents didn't demand that he do things of which he wasn't capable, but they insisted that he do everything of which he was.

Jesus repeated this lesson in several ways. He makes the same point after telling the story of the seed sown in four conditions: "And he answered them, 'To you it has been given to know the secrets of the kingdom of heaven, but to them it has not been given. For to him who has will more be given, and he will have abundance; but from him who has not, even what he has will be taken away'" (Matt. 13:11–12).

It may seem out of character to hear Jesus saying, "From him who has not, even what he has will be taken away." At first glance, it appears unfair. But this is a special case, in that he was referring to a person's inner development. Don't talents indeed wither away if not used regularly? This was what he was getting at. Those who heard and lived by his teachings would receive even more blessings as they practiced these principles and shared them with others. Those who let his Word wither would eventually have a spiritual wasteland inside. Jesus was naming an interesting dynamic that certainly applies to gifts and talents of all kinds. If we, for instance, want more piano-playing talent, we must play the piano. If we never practice, we'll lose any little talent we once had.

Helping Children Develop Special Talents

1. Offer help with what's important to your child. If he wants to make a fort out of cardboard boxes, don't tell him he's making a mess or turning the yard into a disaster zone. Ask him if he needs any supplies. Jesus helped fishermen catch more fish—their occupation—then offered them new challenges.
2. When your child comes to you for praise, focus on her effort ("You've really been working hard on this, haven't you?") and her improvement over her past performance ("I can see you're learning how to draw the cat's head now"). Avoid comparing her performance to that of others ("Wow, this is much better than David's picture!") or overdoing praise. Jesus praised when the time was right.
3. When a child begins to resist some activity, don't say, "You have to finish what you start." Take this opportunity to teach him about commitment by making statements or asking questions such as, "I wonder what makes this not as much fun as before. Do you think it's because you don't like it after all or because what you're learning now is especially difficult?" The goal is to help the child think through his decision to quit before doing so. Your child may realize he was taking those lessons only to please you. *Quitting an activity to which one does not feel "called" and for which one feels no genuine desire to learn is actually a positive action,* for it opens us up to other pursuits for which we will have real interest and passion. Like Jesus, focus on the process of setting priorities and choosing one's path. Compared to children whose parents make decisions for them, the child who learns how to think through his or her choices will more likely make good ones in the future.

The story of the talents is compelling for parents because the master expected each of his three servants to manage the assets given them, not just sit on them. How we, similarly, long to see our children make full use of their talents!

159

"Watch therefore, for you know neither the day nor the hour.

"For it will be as when a man going on a journey called his servants and entrusted to them his property; to one he gave five talents, to another two, to another one, to each according to his ability. Then he went away. He who had received the five talents went at once and traded with them; and he made five talents more. So also, he who had the two talents made two talents more. But he who had received the one talent went and dug in the ground and hid his master's money. Now after a long time the master of those servants came and settled accounts with them. And he who had received the five talents came forward, bringing five talents more, saying, 'Master, you delivered to me five talents; here I have made five talents more.' His master said to him, 'Well done, good and faithful servant; you have been faithful over a little, I will set you over much; enter into the joy of your master.' And he also who had the two talents came forward, saying, 'Master, you delivered to me two talents; here I have made two talents more.' His master said to him, 'Well done, good and faithful servant; you have been faithful over a little, I will set you over much; enter into the joy of your master.' He also who had received the one talent came forward, saying, 'Master, I knew you to be a hard man, reaping where you did not sow, and gathering where you did not winnow; so I was afraid, and I went and hid your talent in the ground. Here you have what is yours.' But his master answered him, 'You wicked and slothful servant! You knew that I reap where I have not sowed, and gather where I have not winnowed? Then you ought to have invested my money with the bankers, and at my coming I should have received what was my own with interest. So take the talent from him, and give it to him who has the ten talents. For to every one who has will more be given, and he will have abundance; but from him who has not, even what he has will be taken away.'"

Matthew 25:13–29

> One thing I know: the only ones among you who will be really happy are those who will have sought and found how to serve.
>
> Albert Schweitzer

We should notice a critical detail of the story: Each servant had the *choice* to do as he wished with his talents (a talent in those days was a form of money). Some choices brought greater returns than others—but the important thing was that two servants tried to develop that which they'd been given. And notice that each person was responsible only for the talents he received, not for those given to the next person. This can be tough for parents to remember. We can be so sure that our child is the best piano player, swimmer, or artist in the world, but our child may disagree! Our child may not even enjoy the skill for which we think he or she has so much talent. The child may be attracted to activities or a career that to us seems unworthy of his or her abilities.

This is where we have to honor the gifts and interests that God gave our child, even if they're not those we would have chosen. Marcus Braybrooke notes:

> The word *gifted* is usually applied to those noted for their creative, sporting, or professional ability. . . . A gift, however, may consist of something less glamorous, but just as valid and necessary for self, community, and even humankind. Teaching, nursing, raising children, listening to others' problems—all these require different but equally valid gifts. Jesus did not indicate a pecking order of spiritual gifts. However, he did insist that whatever gifts people have been given, they should not "bury them in the ground"—that is, waste, hide, or ignore them.[2]

Jesus "parented" his disciples and inspired them, but he didn't push them past their limits or demand that they excel at everything. He gave them a sensible blend of big tasks, such as preaching and healing, and those that they sometimes seemed to consider menial, such as food preparation, as in the story of the loaves and the fishes. Doing the menial is essential in the development of any skill or talent. All those unseen, tedious hours in practice and preparation are what make the great performance possible.

▶ **Lesson 2: Support your child's growth.** How can you realistically help your child triumph over obstacles and develop his or her talents? Jesus coached and mentored his disciples with methods that were part of an overarching approach, which honored their psychological, practical, emotional, and spiritual needs. Jesus, beginning with average persons showing no outward signs of giftedness,

- expressed his belief in and appreciation of them
- taught them in brief "teachable moments" or when they expressed interest
- monitored and coached them through mistakes and failures
- offered opportunities for them to learn, practice, and improve
- praised them for their effort and commitment, not for perfect performance

Try using Jesus' approach with your child. You may want to start with only one or two of the tenets and practice each one over time. Eventually you'll encourage your child's learning and development as Jesus would.

▶ **Lesson 3: Patiently explain and use imagination in teaching.** Anyone who thinks there's no humor in the Scriptures hasn't paid close attention to scenes such as the following, in which Jesus makes a profound statement to his disciples, who quickly huddle together to figure it out. At last they think they know what he meant—they forgot to bring lunch!

> When the disciples reached the other side, they had forgotten to bring any bread. Jesus said to them, "Take heed and beware of the leaven of the Pharisees and Sadducees." And they discussed it among themselves, saying, "We brought no bread." But Jesus, aware of this, said, "O men of little faith, why do you

discuss among yourselves the fact that you have no bread? Do you not yet perceive? Do you not remember the five loaves of the five thousand, and how many baskets you gathered? Or the seven loaves of the four thousand, and how many baskets you gathered? How is it that you fail to perceive that I did not speak about bread? Beware of the leaven of the Pharisees and Sadducees." Then they understood that he did not tell them to beware of the leaven of bread, but of the teaching of the Pharisees and Sadducees.

Matthew 16:5–12

He explained what he had said, and they finally realized he was talking about what the Pharisees and Sadducees were teaching, which spread like leaven (yeast),[3] leading people away from God's priorities and toward human traditions or laws. I always wonder when I see passages like this if Jesus didn't say a little prayer for patience!

The truth is that the disciples did have a hard time understanding some of Jesus' parables. Each time they didn't get it, Jesus explained what he had meant, as he did when they didn't understand the story about the seeds sown in different conditions. As much as those blank looks must have frustrated him at times, Jesus never gave up on them or scolded them. I imagine he did sometimes wonder, however, how they would manage once they were out on their own. We all know that feeling; we say something that seems crystal clear to us, but our child shows no understanding. When we're full of energy, we have no trouble explaining again. It's when we are sleep deprived or stressed that the chore of making ourselves clearer is daunting. Sometimes it's better to delay the discussion for a later time, when both child and parent have more time and energy.

Imagine the scene. After the Pharisees criticized the disciples for eat-

> Advice is like snow; the softer it falls, the longer it dwells upon, and the deeper it sinks into, the mind.
>
> Samuel Taylor Coleridge

163

ing without washing their hands, Jesus defended them by saying that it isn't what goes into the mouth but what comes out of it that defiles a person—hence they, the religious leaders, were defiled by their own motives. The Pharisees were outraged. Then, the minute Jesus and the disciples were alone, they asked what he had meant. "Are you also without understanding?" he asked. "Do you not see?" (15:16–17). Did he sigh then? At any rate, he did go on to explain what he had meant.

This seemed to happen with some regularity. The Samaritan woman at the well—without benefit of schooling—had no trouble understanding him, but his beloved disciples did:

> The woman said to him, "I know that Messiah is coming (he who is called Christ); when he comes, he will show us all things." Jesus said to her, "I who speak to you am he."
>
> Just then his disciples came. They marveled that he was talking with a woman, but none said, "What do you wish?" or, "Why are you talking with her?" So the woman left her water jar, and went away into the city, and said to the people, "Come, see a man who told me all that I ever did. Can this be the Christ?" They went out of the city and were coming to him.
>
> Meanwhile the disciples besought him, saying, "Rabbi, eat." But he said to them, "I have food to eat of which you do not know." So the disciples said to one another, "Has any one brought him food?"
>
> John 4:25–33

Patience and fortitude! That was what Jesus needed and what we need as parents when our words seem to fall on deaf ears. Jesus patiently explained, "My food is to do the will of him who sent me, and to accomplish his work" (v. 34). He knew they meant well; after all, they were worried that he hadn't eaten. But they just couldn't converse with him at his level. This didn't mean they weren't bright; it meant only that they didn't know how to translate his metaphorical language.

Still, it must have occasioned more than a few sighs on Jesus' part. As parents, we can't be blamed for getting exasperated at times. Children often half listen or, within minutes, forget what we tell them. This is where we can learn from Jesus. When a follower didn't get his message one way, Jesus didn't keep hammering him with that same parable over and over again until he understood; rather, he *changed the form* of his message and used it when the next "teachable moment" arose.

Jesus' ability to change the form of his message can be seen, for example, in the many ways he tried to teach the concept of servant leadership. In the Sermon on the Mount, he taught that God values the meek (the humble and gentle) and the peacemakers. When later his disciples were arguing over who would get top billing in the kingdom, Jesus didn't shout, "When will you get this through your heads? I *told* you, the meek will inherit the earth!"

Instead, he gathered *all* of them together (not just the offenders) to discuss the issue in broader terms, describing the kind of behavior, or service, that would make them true leaders. On another occasion, when they were dining at the home of Simon the Pharisee, Jesus used a parable instructing all present to "choose the lower seat" so as not to be embarrassed by being asked to move down to a less prominent position. Yet another time he modeled servant leadership by insisting on washing their feet. Through his symbolic conduct and verbal explanation, he again made the same

> In my observation, in fact, the disciples' most obvious trait seems to be their denseness. "Are you so dull?" Jesus asks, and again, "How long shall I put up with you?" While he is trying to teach them servant leadership, they are squabbling about who deserves the most favored position. Their gnomic faith exasperates Jesus. Much of the time a fog of incomprehension separates the Twelve from Jesus.
>
> Philip Yancey

point: In God's eyes competition and power-seeking would disqualify them as leaders.

As you can see, Jesus changed strategies again and again, *persisting* but not *perseverating*. Perseveration is the continuing use of a strategy that doesn't work. As parents, haven't we all perseverated at one time or another? I remember a mother, waiting with the rest of us outside our children's kindergarten, who excelled in perseveration. I will never forget her daily use of one particular child-management strategy as she watched her toddler climb trees, scale walls, and generally run amok: "Jonathan! Jonathan! Jonathan, no! Jonathan! Jonathan, stop! Jonathan, get down! Jonathan, come here! Jonathan!" Would it surprise you to learn that this strategy never once resulted in Jonathan's stopping, getting down, or coming to her? Little Jonathan had long before realized that his mother simply made those sounds over and over, much as a teakettle whistles or a bird chirps. For both child and parent, perseveration is discouraging and quite maddening!

Jesus recognized that if someone doesn't get it with one method of teaching, they probably won't get it any better by that method the next time around.

The methods by which individual children best learn vary tremendously. Jonathan needed focused attention (not "sideways" attention from a mother absorbed in conversation with other adults), a toy or other distraction to keep him entertained while waiting, and an explanation for why he wasn't allowed to do certain gymnastic feats. Children with learning disabilities may need a tailored approach, and professional help for developing such an approach is available through most school systems today. One child may learn best visually (by reading or through the use of color), another by listening to instructions, and still others through touching or moving around materials. Parents of very active children like Jonathan need tailored approaches for teaching and guiding their children. These approaches must match the way in which the children best learn.

166

The Parent Trap: Methods of Instructing/Explaining That Hinder Growth

Parental baby talk: Baby talk is very cute when spoken by babies. It is less cute when spoken by older children whose parents have gotten into the habit of talking down to them. Baby talk leads to more of the same, which often results in the child being ridiculed by peers. Jesus knew his disciples were immature and frequently didn't understand him, but he took care not to talk down to them. Instead, he explained a concept again or altered his teaching methods to help them understand.

Over-explaining: Jesus taught the disciples a little at a time and stopped once they got distracted and started talking about other things. When parents routinely explain even trivial things down to the last detail, children stop listening or forget the command embedded in the monologue. One mother said, "Rickie, let's not pull the cat's tail, because the cat *needs* his tail, and probably doesn't want to have it pulled, and did you know that a cat's tail has a lot of *nerve endings?* Nerve endings are what carry messages of pain from the body to the brain, so that's why . . ." Rickie, now pulling the tail to test the nerve endings hypothesis, will be sad when Mom grabs the cat, shouting, "Rickie, *you'll never learn!*"

Under-explaining: The well-known "Because I said so!" falls here. Children don't need a dissertation, but they do need to know the reasons behind your decisions. When a parent cuts off a child's attempt to understand her reasoning, she's cutting off the child's budding capacity for thinking things through and understanding the consequences of his or her choices. Jesus routinely explained why he did things, such as why he spoke in parables to the crowds; he wanted his disciples to understand, so they could develop their own methods.

Sham questions: Jesus used questions frequently to get people to reflect on their choices and priorities. Sham questions (questions that are really commands) lead a child to distrust questions altogether. Some adults bristle at even innocent questions, thinking each one is a trap, because questions *were* a trap when they were children. If Dad asks, "Do you want to stop jumping on that table now?" Tony assumes that he has a choice. Tony is shocked and learns to resent questions when Dad suddenly yells, "You never listen! I told you to stop jumping on that table!"

▶ **Lesson 4: Sometimes you'll need to give detailed instructions.** Whenever he was about to give his disciples greater freedom or a new task, Jesus shifted from visionary leadership—inspiring them by offering a vision of what they could achieve one day—to answer-centered leadership—instructing them in practical, detailed ways. When trying something new, we need to be informed, by someone who knows, what lies ahead. The instructions Jesus gave included *practical advice,* for example, to carry nothing with them on their travels.

Another form of instruction was *psychological preparation* for handling disappointments along the way. An instance of this was when Jesus told the disciples simply to "shake the dust from their sandals" when people rejected them. This was a safer alternative, conforming to Jesus' charter, than arguing with those who criticized or rejected them.

> These twelve Jesus sent out, charging them, "Go nowhere among the Gentiles, and enter no town of the Samaritans, but go rather to the lost sheep of the house of Israel. And preach as you go, saying, 'The kingdom of heaven is at hand.' Heal the sick, raise the dead, cleanse lepers, cast out demons. You received without pay, give without pay. Take no gold, nor silver, nor copper in your belts, no bag for your journey, nor two tunics, nor sandals, nor a staff; for the laborer deserves his food. And whatever town or village you enter, find out who is worthy in it, and stay with him until you depart. As you enter the house, salute it. And if the house is worthy, let your peace come upon it; but if it is not worthy, let your peace return to you. And if any one will not receive you or listen to your words, shake off the dust from your feet as you leave that house or town."
>
> Matthew 10:5–14

Sometimes Jesus gave advice that was both spiritual and practical, as when he warned his disciples not to cast pearls before swine, a metaphorical way of saying that they should not try to teach those who clearly don't want to learn, who will trample the precious spiritual wisdom the disciples offer, and who may turn on them physically in anger and harm them. Jesus gave detailed instructions for complex tasks, such as going to get the colt for him to ride into Jerusalem; he even gave the disciples scripts to use in case they encountered questioning or opposition from others. Jesus gave detailed instructions and the words to say when he told two disciples to go find a room in which they could celebrate Passover. Notice his symbolic conduct. He teaches a middle way of guidance, neither leaving a new task entirely up to them nor doing it for them.

> And he sent two of his disciples, and said to them, "Go into the city, and a man carrying a jar of water will meet you; follow him, and wherever he enters, say to the householder, 'The Teacher says, Where is my guest room, where I am to eat the passover with my disciples?' And he will show you a large upper room furnished and ready; there prepare for us." And the disciples set out and went to the city, and found it as he had told them; and they prepared the passover.
>
> Mark 14:13–16

One might well wonder if the disciples could have gotten the colt or reserved the upper room without having been instructed step-by-step in the process. Or even if they had obtained the colt or the room without Jesus' coaching, might they have done so at the cost of making the owners angry or creating other problems by going into the situation with the wrong attitude or words?

Too often we give a child greater freedom or responsibility without adequate instruction, preparation, or coaching. For example, many parents have given their child freedom in terms of planning their own schedules for TV and homework without really discussing how to make a schedule; without providing the appointment book, calendar, or other materials needed; or without discussing the pros and cons of various scheduling choices as they affect the child's homework or fun time.

▶ **Lesson 5: When your children fail, give them permission to try again.**
Jesus predicted failure to inoculate

> Education is the ability to listen to almost anything without losing your temper or your self-confidence.
>
> Robert Frost

169

his disciples against discouragement and self-blame when they failed or encountered obstacles. For instance, when he sent them to preach and heal in various villages and towns, he told them in advance that some people would reject them and their message. After failures did occur, Jesus didn't berate his disciples, nor did he give up on them. After Peter's three denials, Jesus didn't say, "Well, it's pretty obvious you haven't got leadership potential," or "I guess I was wrong about your commitment."

Jesus didn't minimize the failure, but neither did he hold on to it. Jesus interacted with people in such a way that if someone gave up on a goal or talent, it would be because he wanted to, not because he'd been made to feel so condemned about his failures that he didn't dare try again. This was Jesus' secret: The moment the person wished to make another attempt, Jesus was happy to receive him. He continued working with his student from there, *as if no failure had ever happened.* He knew that Peter already felt bad enough; there was no need to rub it in. Who hasn't run headlong into failure at one time or another?

Peter was lucky to have a teacher and mentor who made it clear that failure isn't permanent. John Maxwell sums up the attitude toward failure that Jesus modeled and that we can model for our children:

> After you've been knocked down, and you've had the will to get back up, the intelligence to plan your comeback, and the courage to take action, know this: You will experience one of those defining moments. . . . Prepare for that moment and know it's coming—and you increase your chances for winning your way through it.[4]

> [Adversity is] the state in which a man most easily becomes acquainted with himself, being especially free from admirers then.
>
> Samuel Johnson

The Most Important Lesson

Jesus taught that God calls us not because we're great but because we have the potential to be great. So it was when

170

Jesus selected the Twelve from a larger group of followers. As realtors often say about old houses, one could say that the disciples "needed a little work." The Scriptures are filled with instances of their misunderstandings, anxieties, impulsive words or behaviors, and childish bickering. Yet somehow Jesus managed to help them minimize or compensate for their weaknesses while drawing out talents they (and surely their friends and relatives) never dreamed they possessed.

Sometimes when we're busy with "important" people and things, we can forget that our child, despite all signs to the contrary, needs to talk with us, learn from us, and simply spend time with us. When we talk with children about their thoughts, feelings, and whatever interests them, we're not only supporting them and sharing our wisdom, we're also sending the message that we consider them worthy of attention and capable of learning and growing. Additionally, since children tend to view God much as they do their parents, showing an interest in them boosts their confidence that God too is on their side and wants them to fully develop their unique gifts. And this may be the most important lesson of all.

Remember and Reflect

Did your parents have realistic expectations of you when you were young? Looking back, did *you* expect too much, or too little, of yourself?

What are your special gifts or talents? Do you hide any of them from view out of fear that you may not measure up to the expectations of others or that if people knew, they would expect more of you?

> It is a greater work to educate a child, in the true and larger sense of the word, than to rule a state.
> William Ellery Channing

Did you grow up with encouragement to develop all your gifts? Were people too busy or stressed to help guide you? Did you give up on certain talents too soon?

Does your child see the same talents in himself or herself that you see? How might you help your child recognize what it is he or she truly wants to do or try?

How would Jesus encourage your child right now? What would he see as your child's greatest needs in terms of intellectual, social, or artistic development?

8

Nurturing and Guiding Your Child

"Truly, I say to you, as you did it to one of the least of these my brethren, you did it to me."

Matthew 25:40

Jesus had to actively shepherd his disciples through good times and bad. He was there for them, whether they were tired, angry, frightened, or sad. We who seek to raise our children as Jesus would must be there for them, whether they're making our day or breaking our heart. When we meet our children's many needs—even when some parents would back away or call it quits—we are, Jesus taught, caring for God as well.

With one story about a king who judged his people in a most unusual way, Jesus startled his listeners, teaching that the way they were treating each other was the way they were treating God. Today we're no less shocked. Must we now see God in every face, hear God in every voice?

An impossible standard, some would say. Jesus understood very well that what he asked was possible only with God's help. Certainly we can't follow this standard as parents without frequent prayer and reflection. Even for parents who were raised with great compassion and wisdom and have enormous energy and commitment to their children, there will always be those days when their patience is strained to the limit—hence the colorful saying, "You're standing on my very last nerve!"

For those who wish to raise their children as Jesus would, the teaching that we are to treat them as we would treat God provides a reliable and easy-to-use filter. When we pass our next statements and actions through it before carrying them out, only those that are compassionate, loving, and accepting of the child, and thus of God, will make it through.

Learning from Jesus

We too are "the least of these" to whom Jesus was referring. We've all experienced the pain of being judged, criticized, misunderstood, or treated harshly at one time or another. Such things can make us feel, mistakenly, that we're the only ones who bear these burdens and that no one sees our suffering. Jesus taught that God notices. Whether it's a slap or a kiss, God feels the emotional impact of what people do to one another. Jesus provided an amazingly precise set of guidelines for doing to God by doing to others. If you learn and practice these as a parent, you will give your child the security of feeling truly "seen," understood, and loved.

▶ **Lesson 1: What you do for your child, you do for God.** This is an exceedingly strange and revolutionary idea. Most people think of their behavior toward God as quite separate from their behavior toward others. What does my relationship with God have to do with my response to that irritating coworker, impatient store clerk, or whining child? According to Jesus, everything:

"When the Son of man comes in his glory, and all the angels with him, then he will sit on his glorious throne. Before him will be gathered all the nations, and he will separate them one from another as a shepherd separates the sheep from the goats, and he will place the sheep at his right hand, but the goats at the left. Then the King will say to those at his right hand, 'Come, O blessed of my Father, inherit the kingdom prepared for you from the foundation of the world; for I was hungry and you gave me food, I was thirsty and you gave me drink, I was a stranger and you welcomed me, I was naked and you clothed me, I was sick and you visited me, I was in prison and you came to me.' Then the righteous will answer him, 'Lord, when did we see thee hungry and feed thee, or thirsty and give thee drink? And when did we see thee a stranger and welcome thee, or naked and clothe thee? And when did we see thee sick or in prison and visit thee?' And the King will answer them, 'Truly, I say to you, as you did it to one of the least of these my brethren, you did it to me.' Then he will say to those at his left hand, 'Depart from me, you cursed, into the eternal fire prepared for the devil and his angels; for I was hungry and you gave me no food, I was thirsty and you gave me no drink, I was a stranger and you did not welcome me, naked and you did not clothe me, sick and in prison and you did not visit me.' Then they also will answer, 'Lord, when did we see thee hungry or thirsty or a stranger or naked or sick or in prison, and did not minister to thee?' Then he will answer them, 'Truly, I say to you, as you did it not to one of the least of these, you did it not to me.' And they will go away into eternal punishment, but the righteous into eternal life."

Matthew 25:31–46

No longer can we take our feelings—however valid they may be—out on others with the reassuring thought that they'll forget or that it's okay because everybody does it. *Jesus taught that whatever we do "to the least of these," even our rebellious, moody, or willful child, we are doing to God.*

175

▶ **Lesson 2: When your child is hungry, feed her.** On a literal level, Jesus was saying that we must feed the hungry. Today there are millions of people who can't get enough to eat, yet agricultural scientists recognize that we have the capacity to feed them all, if only enough of us have the desire and the will to do so. All parents are determined to feed their own children; no matter how much or little money they have, they refuse to let their child go hungry. True, we may not feel like cooking, but we do it anyway. We try hard to find healthy foods our child will eat. Indeed, I've never met a parent who didn't worry about his or her child's nutrition. But a child's need for nourishment is not met in physical food alone.

Mother Teresa said that bread quickly satisfies a person's hunger but that many people are "hungry for love." This kind of hunger, she said, is the worst poverty.[1] "But of course I love my child!" many will say. Yes, parents love their children. But does your child feel it? Is there some hunger that isn't satisfied, the hunger for love, understanding, and acceptance?

Many parents try to buy their children's love with cable TV, video games, expensive toys or high-tech gizmos, even swimming pools and sports cars! These are all fun for children and give them a certain status with their friends, but I can tell you, having worked with children who were given these things, that they don't buy love. What they buy is fun, enjoyment, or gratitude at best—or a sense of entitlement at worst. Filling a child's hunger for love, understanding, and acceptance, *this* is what strengthens the connection between parent and child. The trouble is, our culture says, "Just buy this toy/car/investment service/life insurance policy, and your child will

> Listening is a magnetic and strange thing, a creative force. The friends who listen to us are the ones we move toward, and we want to sit in their radius. When we are listened to, it creates us, makes us unfold and expand.
>
> Karl Menninger

176

love you." Having been mesmerized by repeated messages of material goods as the avenue to family harmony, we've all but forgotten how to give—or even find for ourselves—the food that never perishes. Jesus had it, and he knew it: "Meanwhile the disciples besought him, saying, 'Rabbi, eat.' But he said to them, 'I have food to eat of which you do not know.' So the disciples said to one another, 'Has any one brought him food?' Jesus said to them, 'My food is to do the will of him who sent me, and to accomplish his work'" (John 4:31–34).

Jesus' connection with God was so strong, so unfailing, that he felt fed, his spiritual hunger filled. Jesus knew that God truly heard and understood him. This is the kind of connection we can provide for our children, if only we have the desire and the will to do so.

It's sad, however, that "listening food"—by which we nourish someone by listening to him or her without interruption—is rare in families today. It's come to be considered the exclusive domain of therapy, and the unquestioned assumption is that only a highly trained professional can (or will) listen deeply, with a strong focus on the other person. People have come to expect this level of interest, curiosity, and caring only from someone they're paying. I don't believe that this is because people don't *want* to provide these things for their children, their friends, their spouses, and others. I think that as a society we've simply forgotten how.

Jesus knew how. He nourished his disciples and others he met in his ministry with listening food, not the pseudo-listening we're accustomed to, which amounts to:

- You talk for a minute, then I'll tell you whether what you're saying makes sense or not.
- I'll ask you a question, but please realize that there's only one right answer—the one I want to hear.

177

- Briefly share how you're feeling, and I'll say, "I see," or "Uh-huh . . ." and then tell you how *I'm* feeling, what *my* day's been like, and what *I'm* doing tonight.

Jesus' disciples sometimes urged him to press on, and on occasion it may have been more prudent to keep moving in his travels, but again and again he stopped to talk with someone in need, to feed some spiritually hungry person with listening food. We too can feed our children's hunger for attention and understanding by asking how they feel and what they think, then listening without interrupting or becoming distracted. What more nutritious snack can you give your child than listening food?

▶ **Lesson 3: When your child is thirsty, give him something to drink.** I'll never forget the day my youth group went to a North Carolina beach. A few of us went for a walk and soon got lost. We couldn't find our group and had no money with us. For hours we walked in the hot southern sun. Finally, we found the anxious chaperones, who'd come searching for us. We wanderers quickly ran to a drugstore and got in line to order a cold drink. Oh, the agony of waiting in that line! When at last I got my soft drink, I brought it to my lips with trembling hands. That was the most delicious drink in recorded history! I emptied the large cup in seconds and the relief was instantaneous. I felt physically—and mentally—revived. Our brains, which not only think but maintain emotional balance, are about 75 percent water and don't function well without sufficient hydration.

A child at a theme park was crying piteously, "Please, I'm so thirsty!" but his mother never answered him, yanking him along by the wrist. He was suffering, as I was that day on the beach. We all know how it feels when we're unable to quench our physical thirst, but this boy's thirst was for more than just water. He thirsted for someone to care, to respond to his needs.

A parent who is too busy or doesn't realize the importance of tuning in to his or her child often expresses surprise when the child gets into trouble or drops out of school. The child knows, but frequently can't explain, that those "bad kids" he or she hangs out with are like a lifeline. This is the secret pull, not the drug or the crime culture itself. Many young people have told me that they hated the filthy conditions or dangers associated with a drug or gang lifestyle. But for children who don't feel understood, all the unpleasantness and risk in the world is worth the feeling of being seen and heard by someone. Children need their thirst for attention quenched through strong connections with their parents. The connection between child and parent, if strong and consistent, paves the way for the child's lasting connection with God. In that relationship is the living water of which Jesus spoke.

> The Samaritan woman said to him, "How is it that you, a Jew, ask a drink of me, a woman of Samaria?" For Jews have no dealings with Samaritans. Jesus answered her, "If you knew the gift of God, and who it is that is saying to you, 'Give me a drink,' you would have asked him, and he would have given you living water." The woman said to him, "Sir, you have nothing to draw with, and the well is deep; where do you get that living water? Are you greater than our father Jacob, who gave us the well, and drank from it himself, and his sons, and his cattle?" Jesus said to her, "Every one who drinks of this water will thirst again, but whoever drinks of the water that I shall give him will never thirst; the water that I shall give him will become in him a spring of water welling up to eternal life."
>
> John 4:9–14

Through the Spirit, the living water, we and our children will be eternally satisfied. When our children's thirst for meaning, purpose, and a sense of connection with God

> The lonely one offers his hand too quickly to whomever he encounters.
>
> Friedrich Nietzsche

is satisfied, they have no need to look elsewhere for relief. Hence, we must help our children feel connected to us and to God.

▶ **Lesson 4: When your child is a stranger, welcome her.** What does it mean to be a stranger? In a literal sense, Jesus was referring to anyone who is unfamiliar to us. He modeled a welcoming stance to people he met along the road, in small villages or big cities, everywhere. He also made a point of socializing with the "wrong kind" of people, sending a strong message through his symbolic conduct that strangers—the new person, but also the person who seems "strange" to us—were to be accepted and loved, not judged or rejected. Jesus saw every person as God's creation, so he couldn't very well see anyone as a stranger.

Laurie Beth Jones, author of *Jesus, CEO,* notes that Jesus was a very different kind of leader, one who inspired affection and loyalty through spending lots of time with his disciples, his "staff." She writes, "Jesus spent lots of time with his staff. And I wonder whether it wasn't really the picnics and the echoes of his laughter that bound their hearts to him so."[2] Jesus knew that relaxed time with his disciples was essential for inspiring their zeal and dedication and for maintaining a strong connection with them.

Through his parable about the good Samaritan, Jesus instructed people to accept, and even care for, those they consider strange or foreign. Often parents whose children seem different chafe at the idea of accepting them as they are: "But I don't *like* the way my child is!" It certainly is challenging to be accepting when your child is significantly different from you. But to follow Jesus' example, parents must communicate their acceptance of their child as an individual, even while expressing their concerns or setting (reasonable) limits on things like behavior or clothing.

Jesus taught his followers not to judge others and to look first at their own faults before addressing those of others. When we judge we say, "You're totally wrong, so I don't want to even hear your side of the matter." Jesus was *not* forbidding people to address the negative or counterproductive actions of others; he was asking them to examine themselves first to discover what they may have done, or failed to do, that led to the problem.

Few parents would admit that they judge their child, but when they're angry or disappointed, it's natural to look for the cause of their distress. When that cause seems to be their child, they may have thoughts such as, *He's just a spoiled brat. She's grown up to be so trashy. He's a klutz.* These are judgmental thoughts.

For those who want to avoid judging their children (or anyone else), one easy giveaway is the use of any negative statement about the person that includes the words *is, be,* or *are,* because these are "being" words, which *define a person* (thus judging them). Try to make statements with words such as *has* or *have,* which *define a behavior,* not the person. For instance, when her mother says, "Kristi is moody," it sounds as if there's no hope Kristi can change; both mother and Kristi will eventually come to consider this a permanent condition. On the other hand, if her mother changes her wording—"Kristi has some moody behaviors at this time"—the very same problem is described, but now more accurately, and includes the possibility for change.

Jesus knew that judgment is something that closes hearts and

> If we have a clear image of Jesus, we at least know where to start. It is so easy to go wrong and make costly mistakes. So many of us view our relationship with a judgmental God as centered around law. Even those who profess that faith alone saves so often center their spiritual life around the righteous observance of the law, and usually with the rigidity of Old Testament observance, as if they totally missed the spirit of Jesus.
>
> Joseph Girzone

181

minds, leaving no room for redemption or growth. To stop focusing on Kristi's problem and to escape the judgment trap, Kristi's mother should consider her influence on Kristi's behavior. Has she inadvertently modeled some moody behaviors that Kristi has copied, or has she mentioned the moodiness so often that Kristi has taken on this identity, fulfilling her mother's view of her? Kristi's mother may, when she examines her own behavior, discover that her contribution to the problem lies in something ordinarily considered a good thing—getting promoted and working long hours—which cuts short the time she spends with Kristi. Kristi needs time with her mother so that she won't feel so alone (but don't expect her to *admit* she needs more time with Mom). Looking for our own contribution to a problem is more productive and less distressing than looking for ways to blame ourselves (or the other person).[3] Furthermore, when we realize that God forgives our errors as soon as we ask, we need not waste time feeling like a failure but can get on with correcting the situation.

This is the model we want to present to our children so they can face their own failures, make the necessary changes, and move on. As we demonstrate actively our acceptance of our children, we free them to examine themselves and adjust their behavior.

▶ **Lesson 5: When your child is naked, clothe him.** *Of course I clothe my child,* you may be thinking. Many parents wish, however, that they could give their child more clothes or at least nicer clothes. How many parents have felt the pain of being unable to provide their child with the clothes and shoes that "all the other kids are wearing"? This is a hurt that parents hide but that millions experience.

> Do not mistake a child for his symptom.
> Erik Erikson

Clothing keeps us warm and signals how much money we have (or don't have); as such, clothing is both a physical necessity and a shield from shame. A common nightmare that people have when they're feeling anxious involves finding themselves naked in a public place; this is a cue that they're afraid of failing and of others *seeing* them fail. When we clothe the naked, whether with actual clothing or with our words and actions, we protect them from physical *and* psychological harm.

My grandparents were very poor, living in logging camps in the Deep South. Money for food was always hard to come by, and money for clothes was out of the question. So my grandmother (whom I called Sweetheart) became quite a seamstress, sewing all the children's clothing without a pattern, often out of feed sacks or flour bags. You may consider this depressing, and indeed it was a hard life, but poor people are often very resilient.

Sweetheart taught her children to follow Jesus' teachings, which imbued them with a sense of self-worth and equality with others. When it came to appearances, she would emphasize, "One thing's for sure, my children are always clean!" Hair, nails, shoes, clothes, skin—all had to be squeaky clean. As you might expect, this required a lot of time together doing routine things—getting baths, rubbing clothes on the tin washboard, cleaning nails, and braiding hair. My grandmother thus devoted oceans of time to her children, and she "clothed" them with her determination that they feel good about themselves—money or no money.

This emphasis on viewing the world, including themselves, as Jesus would provided a buffer against the teasing that many economically disadvantaged children face. When a child stands out in some way—because he or she is different in terms of body size, learning abilities, clothing, religion, or race—a feeling of being "emotionally naked," too exposed to the world, is common. Parents can help by listening to the child's concerns and talking about his or her special strengths or talents. *Every* child is unique, valuable, and cherished by God, no matter what others may say, and it's up to us as parents to clothe them with this reassurance.

I've worked with high-powered professionals who could buy their children every designer item in the finest boutique, but their children had become distant, depressed, or hostile. These parents first responded to their children's behavior by trying harder and giving their children pep talks or expensive presents. Yet the harder they tried, the more distant and ungrateful their children became! When I have spoken with children from such families, I have seen that they don't want more effort or more indulgence; they want more *parent*. It is hard to convince these over-scheduled parents that their children need a different kind of time with them; they believe in that mystical thing called "quality time."

Searching for an image that would convey what their children most need—relaxed, long stretches of just-being-with time, with no pressure to open up or cheer up—I have finally found one that works. It's the image of a whale, too large for quick turns or fancy moves, just drifting along in the deep ocean waters, her little one swimming with her, side by side, just doing routine daily things, taking their time.

Once these parents slow down, they realize that their children need more of *them*, but in "whale time." They learn to "clothe" their children with side-by-side attention and acceptance, and their children respond over time. In your mind's eye, can't you just see Jesus walking slowly with his disciples down those long, hot, dusty roads, clothing them with oceans of his time and companionship?

▶ **Lesson 6: When your child is sick, care for her.** Jesus likened himself to a physician and spoke like one as well.

> And one of the crowd answered him, "Teacher, I brought my son to you, for he has a dumb spirit; and wherever it seizes him, it dashes him down; and he foams and grinds his teeth and

184

becomes rigid; and I asked your disciples to cast it out, and they were not able." And he answered them, "O faithless generation, how long am I to be with you? How long am I to bear with you? Bring him to me." And they brought the boy to him; and when the spirit saw him, immediately it convulsed the boy, and he fell on the ground and rolled about, foaming at the mouth. And Jesus asked his father, "How long has he had this?" And he said, "From childhood. And it has often cast him into the fire and into the water, to destroy him; but if you can do anything, have pity on us and help us." And Jesus said to him, "If you can! All things are possible to him who believes." Immediately the father of the child cried out and said, "I believe; help my unbelief!"

Mark 9:17–24

How frightening for this father! You can hear his agony, his desperation. As the mother of a child with epilepsy, I empathize with all parents who feel helpless to stop an illness or problem that takes over their son or daughter. In this scene, Jesus seems frustrated at first, wondering aloud why people lack sufficient faith, but then quickly he gets down to business. "Bring him to me," he says. He then asks, "How long has he had this?" This kind of caring and focused attention is what every parent who has a sick child craves. And when the father asks if Jesus can help him, Jesus turns it around: "If you can! All things are possible to him who believes." Jesus didn't tell the father to go home and pray, nor did he say, "Leave the boy here, and I'll take care of it." Rather, he asked the father to use his faith, to answer Jesus' questions, and to collaborate with him to heal his son.

All parents need to have access to good care for their children, regardless of income. They need to be heard and to be treated as collaborators. It's frightening when you need a professional's help yet sense he or she isn't really *listening*. I remember the first neurologist we consulted. He insisted on speaking to my child rather than to me, though my daughter was having so many absence seizures that she couldn't remember his last question, let alone her medical history! Helping profes-

185

sionals, whether in medicine, psychology, or education, aren't much help if they resist collaborating with parents. Young or inexperienced parents may leave the doctor's office with silent misgivings about their child's diagnosis or treatment, yet they go along with it because they don't want to appear difficult by asking too many questions.

Jesus was a master collaborator, healing when people were willing to work *with* him rather than passively receiving his services. He never told a parent, "It's all in your head," or "You're just overly anxious." Dr. Jerome Groopman described a harrowing experience when his child was misdiagnosed with something that would have been fatal had he not questioned the treating physician's judgment.[4] He noted that even *physician* parents encounter trouble, because some pediatricians assume they "know too much" and hence tend to imagine their child has every symptom they studied in medical school. Groopman concludes that parents should ask the questions they need to ask, convey the information the doctor should know, and express any doubts they have—even if this means they'll irritate the medical staff or have to change doctors. He likens the value of doubting what an authority figure says to the theological doubt that Paul Tillich wrote about: "If you are doubting something, then you are thinking about it. That kind of skepticism is part of what it means to be a good doctor to one's patients."[5] Doubt, whether in medicine or religion, isn't the problem; rather, it's our failure to admit and express our doubts. A physician confident enough to hear our doubts inspires our faith, just as a parent who can listen to a child's doubts about religion inspires the child's faith.

Jesus knew that his disciples had doubts and fears from time to time, but he didn't ignore or condemn them; rather, he listened and then reassured them. As parents we must do the same when our children become physically or emotionally ill, by collaborating with helping professionals and reassuring our children that we will take care of them. Jesus taught that by doing so, we are ministering to God as well.

▶ **Lesson 7: When your child is in prison, visit him.** In Jesus' day, you could become a prisoner simply by expressing your beliefs, and your sentence could end in capital punishment, as it did for Jesus. Once a prisoner, you lose your identity and your sense of self-worth. It seems that the whole world has turned against you. Whatever you did that was wrong or merely offensive to others, your inner experience is one of being an outcast, forgotten and abandoned.

Human beings are communal creatures. We can't bear isolation; solitary confinement is a terrible punishment. Jesus knew that the greatest loneliness was that of a prisoner and that any little visit was a great service to that person. Jesus taught that when a person visits a prisoner, he or she is visiting God as well. Having worked with kids in juvenile detention centers, I know that their loneliness is palpable, though many have developed a tough exterior to hide it. Every visit from a relative or friend is a lifeline, something to nourish their spirits and help them hold on a little longer.

There is another kind of prison, with invisible bars—the prison in our own mind. When a child becomes hostile, rebellious, and generally unpleasant to be around, it's tempting to let him just go to his room, shut the door, and stay there. Who wants to be on the receiving end of cursing or criticism? Yet this is precisely when a child needs us most.

Have you ever thought about the mutual imprisonment of prisoners and prison guards? Yes, the guards can go home at night, but the reality is that they too must spend enormous amounts of time in ugly prison buildings. Not only that but they are also required to be vigilant every minute of the day.

Parents are imprisoned too when they become angry and ground their children for excessive periods of time (one man grounded his fourteen-year-old for a whole summer for failing

Latin) or when they give their children the silent treatment—
the mental equivalent of solitary confinement.

Our judgmental or harsh words can imprison us as well.
When our child says outrageous things, we naturally want to
point out where he or she is wrong. This is when we need to
develop the ability to pause, say a little prayer for patience, and
grant the child the right to hold those opinions right now, even
if we disagree. Stephen Covey writes:

> Otherwise, to protect themselves they will put us into a men-
> tal/emotional "prison" in their own mind. And we won't be
> released from this prison until we pay the uttermost farthing—
> until we humbly and fully acknowledge our mistake in not allow-
> ing them the right to disagree. And we must do this without in
> any way saying, "I'll say I'm sorry if you'll say you're sorry."

Covey notes that if you don't allow your child to disagree, your
child will still be suspicious, keeping you "behind these prison
bars, behind the mental and emotional labels they have put on
you that gives them some feeling of security in knowing not to
expect much from you."[6]

Jesus spent time talking with the woman at the well, dined
with prostitutes and tax collectors, and addressed spiritual and
physical healing with lepers. "Jesus went out of his way to
embrace the unloved and unworthy, the folks who matter not
at all to the rest of society—they embarrass us, we wish they'd
go away—to prove that even 'nobodies' matter infinitely to God.
'By loving the unlovable,' said Augustine, 'You made me lovable.'"[7] Show your child a loving God by loving him when he is
least deserving. Visit him in his prison, whether actual or mental. Sooner or later, the ice will begin to crack, and you'll begin to see your beloved child peeking through.

When thinking through your child's needs—whether for reassurance, sup-

> There are some
> remedies worse than
> the disease.
> Publilius Syrus

port, or guidance toward self-discipline—you can feel confident that you're parenting as Jesus would if, before carrying out a plan of action or having a conversation, you put it through the filter of Jesus' remarkable teaching in Matthew 25 about doing to God by doing to others. If you take this teaching seriously, over time you'll find that your typical ways of viewing, responding to, and guiding your children have been *utterly transformed*. And that's what's needed to get "heavenly results."

Remember and Reflect

What did you hunger or thirst for as a child? Was your need satisfied? Who could you count on to fill that need?

Did you ever feel like a stranger in your family or school? If so, what made you feel different? Who helped or comforted you then?

Have you ever felt emotionally naked, exposed to teasing, ridicule, or unwelcome stares? If so, what vulnerable area did you need someone to help you clothe?

Were you ever physically or emotionally sick? If so, were your parents able to comfort you, advocate for you, and collaborate with helping professionals?

> **By learning you will teach; by teaching you will learn.**
>
> Latin proverb

189

Did you ever have a time when you felt imprisoned? What kept you feeling isolated from others? Who helped you through that period?

How would Jesus handle your child's psychological and physical needs at this time? How would he guide you toward meeting them?

9

Living by the Golden Rule

"Do to others what you would have them do to you."

Matthew 7:12 NIV

"Do unto others" evokes images of naturally virtuous people who always do the right thing. Nothing could be further from the truth. Very little in the culture supports this high road, and endless forces support the low road. Consider the popular mottoes: "The best defense is a good offense." "Nice guys finish last." "Do it to them before they do it to you." This chapter will discuss how living by the golden rule will give your children the wiser methods Jesus taught for managing anger, handling conflicts, and growing in maturity and confidence.

In our "in your face" world today, most people have no idea how to handle conflicts without resorting to violence. Little arguments quickly escalate into full-blown battles. Victims of bullying see no way out but to bring a gun to school. Road rage leads to fatal accidents. Parents are worried and rightly so. In our eagerness to look out for ourselves, we have forgotten that there is another way.

It's ironic that so many people who identify themselves as Christians consider Jesus' teachings impractical for the real world. This dismissal of Jesus' teachings is all the more amazing today when youth violence is daily splattered across newspaper headlines. The world's solution—identical to that of Christians who ignore Jesus' charter—is not to step back and reevaluate the ways our children are being taught to handle problems but simply to come down harder on children who fight back to prove their toughness, as they've learned to do from the heroes our culture holds up for them as winners and tough guys. If we don't actively teach a realistic alternative, our children can't be blamed for learning conflict-resolution skills from video games, films, and TV shows glamorizing hot tempers; clever, handsome Machiavellian characters; and good guys who win by behaving just like the bad guys—only more efficiently.

Perhaps we should take a second look at what Jesus had to say about handling conflicts. Perhaps, contrary to popular opinion, there's something there, something that our children desperately need. They certainly won't learn a new way from the world, which has proven that its approach to conflict leads reliably to more of the same.

But of course the practical benefits of getting along with and steering clear of violent people weren't Jesus' primary reasons for teaching and modeling the golden rule. His focus was, as always, on helping people grow the kingdom of heaven within their hearts. Like an air traffic controller, he saw dangers ahead that most people never see—until it's too late. He wanted to steer people clear of internal threats, especially the spiritual deadening that occurs when we're filled with resentments or seek revenge. He wanted so much more for his followers—more joy and peace and greater immunity to all the little arguments and problems that go along with being communal beings. We can help nurture the seed of the kingdom in our children's hearts by exemplifying this teaching, especially at home.

Learning from Jesus

"Are children human?" a comedian once asked. His joke reflected a prevailing image of children as something less than fully human. A friend of mine said, "I've noticed that a lot of people seem to view children as something on the order of small animals that make a lot of noise, like a dog." When we read, "Do unto others," do we include children in those "others"? Jesus didn't say, "Do to adults as you would have them do to you." The only way to help our children learn and practice this principle, without dismissing it because they sense hypocrisy in us, is to practice what we preach, using it with *them* as well.

▶ **Lesson 1: Give your child the blessing of the Golden Rule.** "So whatever you wish that men would do to you, do so to them; for this is the law and the prophets" (Matt. 7:12). This world-famous commandment contains a hidden blessing, yet it is among the most misunderstood statements that Jesus ever made.

As a therapist who's privy to the reasons why many people give up trying to live according to Jesus' teachings or even to behave ethically, I can tell you that the reason the commandment is misunderstood is its missing part. What missing part? Most people think there is an additional clause: "so that men will do likewise to you," but it isn't there. In the Bible there are two versions of Jesus' instruction—one in Matthew and one in Luke. Neither one assures us that if we treat people as we'd like them to treat us, they'll return the favor. Whenever I've pointed this out to someone, the look of surprise on his or her face is quite touching. Most people have

> I have learned that, contrary to those who say the gospel solves our problems, in many ways—justice issues, money issues, race issues—the gospel actually adds to our burdens.
>
> Philip Yancey

193

never realized that this is a unilateral commandment, not a reciprocal one. There's no "deal" here, nor did Jesus make any guarantees that his followers' lives would be any easier if they followed this teaching.

Oddly enough, once people realize that the "guarantee" never existed, they tend to express relief. For years they'd assumed they were doing something wrong because this teaching didn't bring the results it "promised." When they understood its true meaning, they realized reciprocity wasn't promised. Jesus was asking his followers to take the narrow gate, the higher path.

So what about the blessing? This hardly seems like a blessing; it's a hard commandment for anyone, let alone a child, to follow. Yet when we genuinely strive to live by the golden rule, certain things that used to bother us fall by the wayside. Someone was nasty to you today, despite your being polite? Aside from the momentary irritation, there's no need to stew about it, because from Jesus' point of view, you succeeded. Someone betrayed you, and you treated the person as you would like to be treated, yet he or she continued to treat you poorly? You can let this incident go, because you behaved in accordance with your highest values and with Jesus' teaching.

For our children, this outlook is so helpful. They will need instruction to understand that they don't have to fight for their honor or get revenge like all the tough guys and beautiful women of TV and film. I understand the tradition of urging kids to fight back when they're teased or bullied (more on that below); nobody wants his or her child to suffer needlessly, and shows of strength are often touted as the one thing that will stop a bully.

> Not the power to remember, but its very opposite, the power to forget, is a necessary condition for our existence.
>
> Sholem Asch

But look around you. The news isn't good. Mistreated children who are armed not with the golden rule but with fantasies of vengeance picked up

194

from TV or movies may indeed fight back, only to be wounded or killed by a handgun. Parents and teachers must let children know that adults will help them when they're being bullied. More and more schools are offering this invaluable service now that tragedies such as that which happened at Columbine High School have underscored its importance.

Yet for those who want to raise their child as Jesus would, even having the help of adults isn't sufficient. We want to give our child the blessing of *feeling like a success when they practice the golden rule, even when others continue to behave poorly*. We also want them to know that they're not obliged to somehow transform other people by "doing unto them" in order to get them to change, behaving in a more positive or desirable way. People often try to get revenge or make a point because, unconsciously, they're hoping for a radical change in the offending party, who'll say, "I've been a real jerk, haven't I?" or "Wow, you're a lot smarter/stronger/tougher than I thought!"

Jesus never implied that one person could change the heart of another. He promised that we have the power to change and control *our responses* to unkind, unjust behaviors—with God's help. Understanding and teaching this distinction not only will help your child let it go when others behave poorly but may even prevent a tragedy.

▶ **Lesson 2: Immunize your child against permissive attitudes toward rage, conflict, and violence.** Jesus, quoting Isaiah, stated what's really important to God: "Go and learn what this means, 'I desire mercy, and not sacrifice.' For I came not to call the righteous, but sinners" (Matt. 9:13). God's acceptance of our devotion and gifts is dependent on the state of our relationships with others. Without this provision, one could continue to seek God's favor, doing all the right external things and feeling blameless, without first purifying one's heart. Jesus knew that a primary cause of impure thoughts and feelings is hostility or conflict, both of which are usually the result of someone hurting, betraying, or angering us. He taught a new, higher standard for handling anger and destructive urges, requiring not only restraint but reconciliation as well.

> "You have heard that it was said to the men of old, 'You shall not kill; and whoever kills shall be liable to judgment.' But I say to you that every one who is angry with his brother shall be liable to judgment; whoever insults his brother shall be liable to the council, and whoever says, 'You fool!' shall be liable to the hell of fire. So if you are offering your gift at the altar, and there remember that your brother has something against you, leave your gift there before the altar and go; first be reconciled to your brother, and then come and offer your gift."
>
> Matthew 5:21–24

Jesus instructed people to settle disputes quickly before they escalated and led to more trouble. He knew that conflicts are inevitable but can poison relationships and derail the best missions (such as Jesus' ministry, a group's commitment, or a person's calling) unless handled with the right attitude and approach. He also knew that smoldering anger often leads to actions resulting in legal charges; then, as now, the poor should not expect to win if pitted against someone with money and connections in a court of law: "Make friends quickly with your accuser, while you are going with him to court, lest your accuser hand you over to the judge, and the judge to the guard, and you be put in prison; truly, I say to you, you will never get out till you have paid the last penny" (vv. 25–26).

Jesus taught people not to resist an evil person but to turn the other cheek, give more when asked for one thing, and go that extra mile:

> "You have heard that it was said, 'An eye for an eye and a tooth for a tooth.' But I say to you, Do not resist one who is evil. But if any one strikes you on the right cheek, turn to him the other also; and if any one would sue you and take your coat, let him

have your cloak as well; and if any one forces you to go one mile, go with him two miles. Give to him who begs from you, and do not refuse him who would borrow from you.

"You have heard that it was said, 'You shall love your neighbor and hate your enemy.' But I say to you, Love your enemies and pray for those who persecute you, so that you may be sons of your Father who is in heaven; for he makes his sun rise on the evil and on the good, and sends rain on the just and on the unjust. For if you love those who love you, what reward have you? Do not even the tax collectors do the same? And if you salute only your brethren, what more are you doing than others? Do not even the Gentiles do the same? You, therefore, must be perfect, as your heavenly Father is perfect."

Matthew 5:38–48

Why did he say these things? Jesus cared not only about the physical danger inherent in resisting people whose hearts and minds are filled with evil thoughts, but the *spiritual danger* as well. Actively resisting an evil person brings out the worst in us, remodeling us in the evil person's image. It seems likely that Jesus was also giving a *practical* instruction to his followers, one that could save their lives. Jesus and his disciples had many enemies, people who were looking for a good excuse to arrest or attack them. Jesus knew that his followers had no political or military clout. What would happen if they resisted a hostile person who did?

It may well be that we do not need to choose between these two interpretations of this saying of Jesus. It may well be that both were in his mind, and that what Jesus is saying is: "If you want happiness in time, and happiness in eternity, never leave an unreconciled quarrel or an unhealed breach between yourself and your brother man. Act immediately to remove the barriers which anger has raised."[1]

An important benefit of this teaching has to do with its "naming" function. It gave the disciples something—evil—to look out for, to recognize when they saw it, and to take special precautions against. This process isn't as simple as it sounds; usually we don't analyze our anger to see what lies behind it.

When you're angry with someone for behaving unjustly toward you, certainly you think the person has done wrong, but deep inside you wonder, *How could he do this to me?* The very act of getting angry suggests that you don't consider the person troubled or afflicted with sin. If you did, you'd move quickly from your initial irritation, hurt, or anger to the sad realization that this behavior signals spiritual problems in that person. If a bee stings you, you might get angry for a moment, but that feeling quickly fades because you know that stinging is just part of being a bee. You know that the sting was motivated by the bee's instincts, not by anything you did or failed to do.

When someone behaves in an unjust or cruel way toward us, we are wise to first examine our own behavior, as Jesus taught, to see if we contributed to the problem through our own blindness or hardness of heart. Then and only then can we look at the other person's behavior and try to understand what motivated it. Sometimes, as we can help our children understand, people are overtired, stressed, or grumpy—but sometimes, as Jesus taught, a person is succumbing to temptation, behaving in ways that Jesus would call sinful or evil. Becoming aware of these realities can help children better cope with their own anger when others have been unkind to them.

Teaching our children to "turn the other cheek" *doesn't* mean they can't address the problem they're having with another person. The lessons of Matthew 5 help them understand the problem as a symptom of their opponent's sinful spirit. This is powerful, because it allows children to *walk away* from conflict, realizing that the hostile person is troubled or, as Jesus said, evil—currently under the control of evil thoughts.

Fighting should be reserved for genuine self-defense in the face of imminent attack, when no other help is available. Preemptive strikes and aggression disguised as self-defense won't pass muster under the golden rule. Fighting to settle a score or make a point will only bring on more conflict, more violence, and more spiritual *and* physical danger.

Lesson 3: Teach and model Jesus' new system for handling conflicts. Jesus taught how to address a problem when we believe someone has wronged us or we have a conflict with someone. You and your child can learn and practice Jesus' system whenever your child is having a problem or conflict with someone. It is usually appropriate for the parent, rather than the child, to initiate the system.

"If your brother sins against you, go and tell him his fault, between you and him alone. If he listens to you, you have gained your brother. But if he does not listen, take one or two others along with you, that every word may be confirmed by the evidence of two or three witnesses. If he refuses to listen to them, tell it to the church; and if he refuses to listen even to the church, let him be to you as a Gentile and a tax collector."

Matthew 18:15–17

Jesus' Five-Step System

1. *Jesus advised his followers to first talk the problem over with the offending person.* If the conflict is mild and your child trusts the other child, he or she may be able to straighten out the problem without help. When your child is upset or anxious, you may need to call the offending child's parent. This may solve the problem right away. Sometimes the child doesn't realize that his or her behavior hurt your son or daughter. Often, however, meanness or selfishness is a carryover of feelings that begin at home through abuse or neglect. Have compassion for the other family, but state clearly the impact that the behavior is having on your child.

2. *Jesus said that if the other person doesn't listen, we should go again to express our concerns, this time with several other people.* I used this system when facing a problem at my child's elementary school many years ago. The lunchroom had become an extremely stressful environment. A monitor had been hired to maintain total silence while the children were eating. If any child whispered to a friend, laughed,

or even coughed too loudly, the monitor would make the child do an exhausting number of jumping jacks or push-ups, military style, in front of all the children. My eight-year-old daughter came home crying when this was instituted; every day when she got home, she released the pent-up stress from sitting, too fearful to eat, and seeing children yelled at and humiliated during what should have been a restful lunch break. After observing this craziness for myself, I discussed my concerns with the new principal, but he wasn't budging. He said the reason for the imposed silence was that the acoustics of the cafeteria were bad. So I called some other parents, and four of us made our case in his office. Promptly the policy was changed. Clearly Jesus knew what he was talking about. When one person hits a brick wall, a group can dismantle it and build something better. Parents must take responsibility for following these steps in difficult situations because children are not yet skilled enough in handling conflicts to proceed on their own. By working with the system using these steps, however, a parent is modeling a reasonable, effective way of solving interpersonal problems—Jesus' way.

3. *If going with others and stating the concern doesn't work, Jesus said to then bring it to the church itself.* Had the principal not listened to us, we parents were prepared to take our case to the PTA. An auditorium full of concerned parents surely would have convinced the principal to change his new policy. A parent whose child was being bullied and who had already tried to talk with the teacher and the other child's parents could bring the problem to the principal. If the bullying was still a problem after that, the parent could call the school board and ask how to proceed.

4. *Jesus said that if even this doesn't work, it's time to give up on the offending party; you've tried your best.* When Jesus said, "Let him be to you as a Gentile and a tax collector," he was referring to people whose hearts are not in the right place, who cannot be reasoned with because they are unprincipled. I've spoken with parents who have removed their children from a school because their concerns were ignored (though rarely have these parents followed Jesus' five-step system). Some parents who can't afford private school have even moved to another location, offering their children a fresh start in a new school district. What a shame to have to do that! But it's far better than allowing a child to continue to suffer from constant teasing, bullying, or outlandish situations like that described above.

5. *Finally, Jesus teaches forgiveness.* "Take heed to yourselves; if your brother sins, rebuke him, and if he repents, forgive him; and if he sins against you seven times in the day, and turns to you seven times, and says, 'I repent,' you must forgive him" (Luke 17:3–4). Jesus told Peter to forgive his brother seventy times seven and told the story of the

servant whose huge debt was forgiven by the king, yet the servant wouldn't forgive a small debt owed to him by someone else (Matt. 18:21–35). The message is that God has forgiven us so many times and for so much that we shouldn't even question the number of times we are to forgive others.

This step is last for a reason. After going through all the former actions to no avail, you and your child are bound to be tired and more than a little angry or resentful. This will weigh you down and, over time, separate you from God. So Jesus taught us to let it go, to forgive, not because what the offending person did was okay but because your spiritual life and happiness are more important.

▶ **Lesson 4: Like Jesus' parents, nurture your child's spirit as you protect and guide him or her to maturity.** When Jesus' parents couldn't find him and finally tracked him down in the temple, they appealed to the safety issue, not the obedience issue. They respected his theological questions and sincere desire to discuss these issues with religious leaders but needed to protect him. It's amazing how rarely the import of this incident is discussed; it's routinely glossed over with no mention made of the fact that Jesus, by not first asking permission, *scared his parents half to death!* This was a *big deal.* Just imagine your reaction if you could not find your child for three days, traveling on long dusty roads from town to town in an age of no telephones or police stations! It seems wise to take a closer look at the way Jesus' parents handled this extreme case, for going one's own way at the age of twelve, without first asking one's parents, even for the very best of reasons, would terrify and anger any loving parent. When Jesus' parents finally found him at the temple back in Jerusalem, they didn't punish him, but they certainly expressed their anguished worry and their need to know his motivation.

Every year his parents went to Jerusalem for the Feast of the Passover. When he was twelve years old, they went up to the Feast, according to the custom. After the Feast was over, while his parents were returning home, the boy Jesus stayed behind in Jerusalem, but they were unaware of it. Thinking he was in their company, they traveled on for a day. Then they began look-

201

ing for him among their relatives and friends. When they did not find him, they went back to Jerusalem to look for him. After three days they found him in the temple courts, sitting among the teachers, listening to them and asking them questions. Everyone who heard him was amazed at his understanding and his answers. When his parents saw him, they were astonished. His mother said to him, "Son, why have you treated us like this? Your father and I have been anxiously searching for you."

"Why were you searching for me?" he asked. "Didn't you know I had to be in my Father's house?" But they did not understand what he was saying to them.

Then he went down to Nazareth with them and was obedient to them. But his mother treasured all these things in her heart. And Jesus grew in wisdom and stature, and in favor with God and men.

Luke 2:41–52 NIV

His mother "treasured all these things in her heart." Here was a mother who saw the promise in her son and had no desire to "teach him a lessson" by physically hurting or threatening him, as some misguided people advise parents to do. She wanted to keep him safe and guide him to adulthood while nurturing his spirit and *guiding* his will. She quietly believed that God had great things in mind for her son, and as time went by, he "grew in wisdom and stature." What might have resulted had Jesus' parents taken the worldly approach, lashing out and humiliating him to shape his will and break his spirit?

Jesus' parents were wiser than worldly parents, believing that God cherished their son, whose independent mind and spirit should not be broken but channeled as he grew into greater maturity and eventually pursued his special calling. What great thing does God have in mind for your child? Can you see sparks of what God sees beneath the ordinary appearances and immature behaviors of childhood? Can you see that diamond in the rough?

▶ **Lesson 5: Treat your children as you want them to treat you and others.** Jesus' disciples often said things that were distressing to him. They asked him for special favors, knowing how he felt about competitive power grabbing. Feeling rejected and angry, they once asked if it would be okay if they prayed for God to wipe out a whole town (Luke 9:54)! They often took him literally when he was speaking metaphorically, asking questions that reflected their inattention, incomprehension, or both. Yet never, with the exception of one topic—when Jesus spoke about his death and they feared asking what he meant—did they seem to feel they couldn't ask or say whatever was on their minds. Think back to all the teachers and bosses you've worked under and ask yourself: *With how many of those people did I feel completely comfortable saying or asking whatever was on my mind?* Probably not many. Why? Because most people in authority positions think their job is to tell not ask, to punish not guide, to talk not listen. Hence they do a pretty bad job of helping those under their supervision to learn and grow.

Jesus took a different approach. He was quite aware of certain behavior problems in some of his disciples but was more concerned with the inner spirit *leading* to those problems. When your focus is on fostering *internal* growth, punishments and other short-term solutions just don't cut it.

Jesus apparently did not put extreme pressure on [Peter] to control his impulsive outbursts during all those years they were together. He knew he would in time, when he had grown to the point where it would happen naturally as an outflow of his inner spirituality. Just to stop for the sake of externals, to create a better impression, would have had little meaning to Jesus. For Jesus, goodness had to flow from the heart.[2]

> You have not converted a man because you have silenced him.
>
> John Morley

Externally focused punishments, such as yelling, slapping, harshly

203

criticizing, and spanking are easy to administer and require no thought or planning. Adults tend to accept however they were treated as children as natural or tradition. But those who seek to raise their child as Jesus would must question these traditions. Is hitting or yelling at a child any way to guide him or her toward the higher path that Jesus urged us to take when he taught the golden rule?

I once witnessed a teacher furiously spanking a tiny preschooler who was paralyzed on the right side of her body. The child had called out, "Daddy!" when a car that looked like his passed the classroom window. As the old saying goes, "What goes around comes around." The way we treat our children is very likely the way they'll treat others one day—and maybe even us—if not physically then verbally.

We often hear complaints about today's permissive parents. But experts on violence see a far more ominous type of permissiveness, the kind that parents and even educators in some states practice, leading to forms of discipline that breed rage in children and are antithetical to the golden rule. Dr. Aaron Beck writes: "Our knowledge of the aberrations of power-driven leaders and their naïve followers needs to be expanded . . . corrective programs need to be directed at the kind of beliefs that justify violence: egocentrism and group egoism; punishment and retribution; diffusion of responsibility; *permissive attitudes toward violence*" (emphasis added).[3] And where do we get this permissiveness toward the use of physical violence as a means to get people to do as we wish? Certainly a great deal of it trickles down as habit from generation to generation, but we mustn't overlook the role of the media.

The rich and powerful of Hollywood and the video game industry have silenced parents' concerns about outrageously violent films, television programming, and video games. Any parent who states his or her con-

What's done to children, they will do to society.

Karl Menninger

204

cern about the graphic violence, often coupled with sexual scenes, broadcast on multiple stations throughout the day is silenced with the old standby response, "Well, all you have to do is turn the TV off," accompanied by the unspoken jab, *like good parents do*. But think about it. Even if you were to prevent your child from ever watching a minute of television, at your home or their friends' homes (and how likely is that?), what about *all those other children and teens* who are watching it endlessly? Many of these children are emotionally troubled and feel a sense of catharsis when viewing violence. Many of them attend your child's school or live nearby. And some of them have access to handguns.

How would Jesus respond to the argument that violent programming must be permitted during the hours that children are watching TV? How would he protect children from the hypnotically repeated message, on the small screen as well as the silver screen: "Do to others as you please, as long as you're bigger, stronger, or have more ammo"?

The combination of permissive attitudes toward violence, too little time spent with overworked parents, and counterproductive parenting methods can cause some children to develop narcissistic, selfish, or vengeful attitudes and behaviors toward others. They've become self-obsessed, which prevents them from respecting, much less observing, the golden rule. What parents need today is the firm but gentle form of shepherding that Jesus used to guide his disciples away from worldly or immature attitudes and behavior, while keeping strong their connection with him. This kind of guidance is entirely unfamiliar to many parents, who have neither experienced it nor witnessed it. A list of books that teach this kind of guidance—the kind that reinforces rather than contradicts the golden rule—can be found in the Suggested Reading section of this book. Parents also must confront the societal forces working against the safety of our children. In fact, we can use Jesus' method for handling conflict, collectively stat-

205

ing our concerns about violent television programming and ads that sexualize children and young teens. We can and should advocate for more responsible use of that highly influential medium.

Walking the Talk

Until my first child was four years old, we lived in a mobile home park. I was considered a novelty there because I didn't spank my child. Several other mothers, with whom for a time I took late-afternoon walks with the children, carried switches and belts to keep their kids in line. They had to admit that my child listened and obeyed more readily than did theirs but chalked it up to fate, not different guidance strategies. "You're just lucky; she's different," they would say. I disagreed; my child could be just as fussy or uncooperative as any other. The difference was that I was reading every book I could get my hands on that taught me how to guide her gently and firmly—more like the shepherding that Jesus modeled and taught than the smacking and threatening my friends used.

The truth is that I had learned to be less permissive than they were. Such methods, I learned, require that parents really communicate with their child and call a halt to irritating or dangerous behaviors *when they first begin* (see the Suggested Reading list at the end of this book). Parenting with firm guidance instead of punishment requires that the parent, like the captain of a ship, keep a watchful eye for potential problems, nipping them in the bud before they become full-blown. My friends, on the other hand, would keep talking to one another and to me, ignoring what their children were doing until somebody got hurt, a big mess was made, something **Spare the rod and** got broken, or things got entirely out of **guide the child.** hand. Then came the screaming, the

206

spanking, the crying, and other miseries I'd just as soon live without. This was repeated with no improvement in behavior, day after day. As much as I liked these women personally, I stopped walking with them because I couldn't stand the inevitable dramatics!

My goal was to have a strong connection with my child so that she would trust me to set limits *only* when they were truly necessary and thus be willing to abide by them when I did. And she did, as did my next child. But I had to *really work at this*. I was young and temperamental; calm responses did not come naturally to me. Yet over time I developed greater self-control and the ability to step back and soothe myself when things got stressful. One day I realized, with great joy, that it no longer even *occurred* to me to yell or spank. This isn't a matter of believing in one approach or another, nor is it a matter of having some kind of magic or special talent. It's a matter of how important it is to us to raise our children as Jesus would, which is never as easy as raising them as our neighbors would.

The golden rule is especially vulnerable to disregard by our children if it's taught but not modeled. If you treat your child harshly yet teach him or her to "do to others as you would have them do to you," your words will fall on deaf ears. Such a child hears flowery ideas but sees something very different in action, and that symbolic conduct—especially since it comes from the crucial role of parent—will make the greatest impact. Such a child will, at best, learn to say the right things while not bothering to put them into action. At worst, he or she will store up rage, resentment, and self-loathing until one day the child explodes violently at someone. Jesus did not say, "Think to others," or "Intend to do to others"; he said, "Do to others." We, the chosen ones who are shepherding the new generation, must model this behavior toward others—including our children—for, as always, our actions speak far louder than our words.

207

Remember and Reflect

As you were growing up, what was the philosophy by which most people around you lived? Was it similar to the golden rule or something altogether different?

Were you ever teased or bullied as a child? If so, how did you handle it? Did your parents or teachers help? How did those experiences affect your personal philosophy about "doing to others"?

Did your parents treat you as they hoped you would treat them? Name some ways in which they did. Now list some ways in which they didn't.

Have you treated your own children as you'd like them to treat you? When you set limits or set up a behavior/consequence contract, is it fair, the kind of thing you wouldn't have minded abiding by at their age?

What would most concern Jesus right now about your child's relationship with you or with others? How would he shepherd your child in that area?

10

Transforming Your Family to Transform the World

"You are the light of the world."

Matthew 5:14

Jesus didn't provide excuses for not sharing your light. He was quite specific. If you have a light—the light that comes from faith and wisdom—you have not just the right but the duty to share it with others. Mistakes, error, sin, failure, none of these exempt us from sharing what we can with others. It may be a tiny flicker at first, but a flicker in darkness is always welcomed. There are people who have no light, and thus we must share what we have.

You may recognize the talents that God has bestowed on you—even if you've not yet put them to use—and feel connected spiritually with God, sure of your footing in terms of understanding and embodying Jesus' teachings. If so, you're at a point in your life when you are feeling the desire to share your light with your children, your friends, your community, perhaps even the world. If not, you may be thinking, I *am the light of the world? Who are we kidding?* Maybe you're confused, irritable, or overwhelmed too much of the time. Maybe you're working so hard that you don't have time to share your light. Maybe you're busy just trying to make a living. Maybe your child has gotten into trouble or seems to hate you lately. Or maybe you're just waiting to become more or less perfect before daring to consider yourself the light of the world.

You are already undergoing a *personal* transformation as you begin to question how Jesus would raise a child. As you reflect and remember how you were raised, you are imagining how Jesus might have done some things differently, had he been your parent. You're discovering how intently Jesus focused on a person's internal life—the soil in which the kingdom of heaven could be sown and nurtured—rather than on external appearances.

Learning from Jesus

▶ **Lesson 1: The more you learn and grow, the more you can share your light with your child and others.** When Jesus told his disciples that they were the light of the world, surely they felt honored, yet I imagine they also experienced a flash of anxiety. All along, they'd seen themselves as Jesus' *followers*, working safely under his tutelage, in his shadow. They knew, all too well, their many weaknesses. Wasn't Jesus the light of the world?

"You are the light of the world. A city on a hill cannot be hidden. Neither do people light a lamp and put it under a bowl. Instead they put it on its stand, and it gives light to everyone in the house. In the same way, let your light shine before men, that they may see your good deeds and praise your Father in heaven" (Matt. 5:14–16 NIV). A frequently missed but essential point here is that Jesus was again *calling* his disciples, this time to begin seeing themselves in a new way. Just when we think we've done all we can do, God bids us to rise and do more. Mother Teresa described her own realization that God wanted

210

her to help the poorest of the poor, which meant leaving the comfortable private girl's school at which she'd taught for two decades, as "a call within a call."[1]

During his years of teaching and healing, Jesus had shouldered the responsibility for sharing his light, first with his disciples, then with vast numbers of people. He knew that his followers were in training, still developing and in need of support and guidance. He saw that they were making progress, despite their inevitable mistakes and wrong turns. Nonetheless, though he foreshadowed their future roles as spiritual leaders, he accepted primary responsibility for spreading his message while the disciples were growing and maturing. "Jesus said, 'As long as I am in the world, I am the light of the world' (John 9:5). When Jesus commanded his followers to be the lights of the world, he demanded nothing less than that they should be like himself."[2]

Jesus' disciples could have shared what they'd learned with their families and left it at that. They could have returned to their former occupations with the reassuring knowledge that they and their families would benefit from Jesus' message. They thereby would have avoided a lot of trouble, expense, and danger. Had Jesus not charged them with spreading their light, and had they not heroically said yes to this "call within a call," his teachings may well have been lost to all humanity.

Jennie, whose family life was painful and lonely because of her father's alcoholism and her mother's depression, became increasingly listless during the first few months at her new school. She kept her head down and avoided her peers as much as possible. One day she came to her chorus teacher, Ms. Bartlett, telling her she needed to be excused because she didn't feel well. Ms. Bartlett was about to ask her why when she saw a small tear in the corner of Jennie's eye. "Is something wrong?" she asked, and a wellspring of tears erupted.

It would have been easy to send Jennie to the nurse's office, with a note referring her to the guidance counselor. Ms. Bartlett

211

did refer Jennie to counseling, but she went beyond the standard response. Taking seriously Jesus' command to share one's light with others, Ms. Bartlett asked Jennie if she'd like to stay after school one day a week for voice coaching. Jennie agreed and every Monday Jennie came for her lesson, standing dutifully beside the grand piano as Ms. Bartlett sat ready to play the music and teach. But every Monday Ms. Bartlett spent about ten minutes on coaching and fifty minutes on nourishing Jennie with listening food. She knew that what Jennie most needed wasn't voice lessons.

Ms. Bartlett never criticized Jennie's parents for their lack of attention to Jennie but empathized with Jennie's suffering. Over a period of months, as Jennie began to respond to Ms. Bartlett's care, she slowly began to come out of her shell. The coaching sessions were soon 50 percent singing and 50 percent talking. By the end of the school year, no longer emotionally and spiritually starving, Jennie was receiving fifty minutes of coaching and ten minutes of listening. Years later Jennie wondered why Ms. Bartlett hadn't demanded that she get down to business and stop talking and sometimes crying. The reason was simple. Ms. Bartlett wanted to guide others as Jesus would and took seriously his mandate to share her light with those in need.

> **Lesson 2: Your light may be inspiring and lifesaving to someone.** Even if you share your light in little ways, it has the potential to offer healing to others. For instance, to critical, punitive parents, you can model a more accepting or nonviolent attitude with your child. You can give messages of warmth and acceptance to cold or rejecting parents. Or you can

What I regret the most is that none of us ever talked with you, Sidda— or Little Shep, Lulu, or Baylor. We hid behind some archaic belief that you do not interfere with another person's children.

Rebecca Wells, from
Divine Secrets of the Ya-Ya Sisterhood

simply spend some time, even a few minutes, talking with a child who's having trouble at home or seems depressed: "A light is often the warning which tells us to halt when there is danger ahead. . . . one of the most poignant tragedies in life is for someone, especially a young person, to come and say to us, 'I would never have been in the situation in which I now find myself, if you had only spoken in time.'"[3]

The hardest task with respect to other people's children is to know how to get involved in times of trouble. To follow Jesus' example, we must speak with parents or to concerned people in the community when we suspect child neglect or abuse.

Lisa Steinberg, a six-year-old girl, was beaten by her adoptive father until, on one terrible night in 1987, she died. Several people had heard the screams or seen the bruises; some had attempted to help her, but eventually the matter was turned over to the social services system. The system failed her, as systems often do, under the weight of its own slowly turning, bureaucratic machinery. Children are abused, neglected, and murdered so often that it's vital for us to ask the question, What would Jesus have done? It's difficult to imagine him being satisfied with "Well, a father has the right to discipline his child as he pleases within the privacy of his own home." Would he have accepted "We'd love to help, but our hands are tied"?

"Leave her alone!" Jesus said in no uncertain terms, thus risking his own life, when he saw men about to stone a woman who'd been accused of adultery. To do likewise when a child is being harmed requires heroism and can save two lives—the child's and the troubled parent's.

Certainly we hope never to be confronted with a case of serious child abuse. But it isn't at all infrequent that we see well-meaning par-

> The ultimate measure of a man is not where he stands in moments of comfort and convenience, but where he stands at times of challenge and controversy.
>
> Martin Luther King Jr.

213

ents who are inadvertently harming their children. What would Jesus do in such cases? How would he have us share our light—that which we've learned from his teachings and example? I must admit that the best example I have of an intervention that signaled a Jesus-like concern regarding a parent's behavior was one that I experienced when I was a young mother.

At twenty-two, living in our small mobile home, I juggled parenting my toddler with college homework in the afternoons and working in a department store in the evenings. It seemed that I was always in a hurry or tired or both. On one particularly stressful afternoon, I heard a knock at the door. I opened it, and there stood the fifteen-year-old girl who lived next door. She looked furtively at me for a moment, then said, "Is everything all right in here? I heard shouting." I felt a flash of righteous indignation and defensiveness. "Everything's fine!" I snapped.

But then my brain kicked in. I realized that this young girl was doing a very brave thing, confronting an adult because she was concerned for my child. And then I thought, *She cares about my daughter, whom I love too.* This teenager wasn't *against* me; she was *for* my child. I softened and realized that indeed I was overtired and had been shouting in an uncontrolled and immature way at my noisy toddler. It was galling because I was taking a child psychology course at the time and expected better of myself. But this was a valuable lesson in humility. "Well, everything's okay now," I said softly. "And . . . thanks." As she left, it occurred to me that she hadn't once accused me of anything; she'd just signaled her concern. She hadn't been angry or arrogant, but neither had she turned a blind eye to the problem.

> It is the heart always that sees, before the head can see.
>
> Thomas Carlyle

That day was a turning point for me. I resolved to get my frustration level under control and begin to take better care of my own needs. Praying for help, strength, and wisdom, I turned my life around in just a few

214

weeks. That's a quick change for a behavior that had become habitual; I can account for it only by referring to what Jesus said—that which is impossible for human beings is possible with God.

▶ **Lesson 3: It's okay if parents or children come for the "free food."** Some parents may become interested in parenting as Jesus would only because they have a pressing problem that they haven't been able to solve any other way. The lesson here is that God will bless even those who come for what they need at the time:

> So when the people saw that Jesus was not there, nor his disciples, they themselves got into the boats and went to Capernaum, seeking Jesus.
> When they found him on the other side of the sea, they said to him, "Rabbi, when did you come here?" Jesus answered them, "Truly, truly, I say to you, you seek me, not because you saw signs, but because you ate your fill of the loaves. Do not labor for the food which perishes, but for the food which endures to eternal life, which the Son of man will give to you; for on him has God the Father set his seal."
>
> John 6:22–27

These people had come for the free food, not Jesus' message! Yet he didn't end the conversation there but used the opportunity to call them and, in so doing, to bless them. You may know a stressed-out parent or a troubled child or teenager who is not interested in anything even close to religion. Jesus never pressured anyone, so we mustn't either. However, we can follow Jesus' example by *inviting* people to spend time with us or to accompany us to worship services. They may refuse, but they'll get the message that we care, especially if we leave it at, "Well, if you do want to come anytime, just let me know." We can introduce them to something that's fun, such as the social or outdoor activities offered by active youth programs or, if they're parents, to upbeat, supportive parenting groups. You never know how much your invitation and kindness could mean to someone.

Just this summer, Sean, a seven-year-old boy, began attending a nearby church's Bible school. Nobody knew him; he looked down a lot and didn't seem too interested in what was going on. Some wondered if his parents might be bringing him every evening just for the free child care. Anything is possible. But one thing was certain. This boy needed something. Jim, one of the teachers, took extra time with him, assigning important tasks to him and asking for his help from time to time. Sean never did interact much with the other kids, but he began to look and smile at Jim. During the lessons, Jim made sure that he gave Sean a lot of eye contact and joked with him between activities. Sean even raised his hand a few times on the last evening and seemed interested in what he was learning about Jesus.

When the week was over, Jim wondered if his efforts would have any lasting impact, since Sean never came to church after Bible school ended. In truth, it doesn't matter if Sean *was* brought for the free child care. Real needs, inner needs, were met. Whatever happens, Sean's spirit has already been changed; a spiritual seed has been planted in at least one spot of good soil, which Jim's kindness and attention had prepared.

Jesus himself took advantage of that kind of "free food" motivation to call and bless people. If we can get parents or kids involved in spiritual training for any reason (I overheard two boys telling their pastor that their youth group had fallen apart due to a dire shortage of girls!), God will take it from there.

▶ **Lesson 4: Little by little, begin living out what you've learned.** A recent newspaper letter to the editor claimed that Christianity has the great advantage over other religions of not requiring any actual changes in its followers: "God requires only faith in His Son, and salvation is secure," the letter writer confidently concludes. "My faith does not depend on what I do, but on what God already has done for me through Jesus."

But what would Jesus say?

"Truly, truly, I say to you, he who believes in me will also do the works that I do; and greater works than these will he do, because I go to the Father. Whatever you ask in my name, I will do it, that the Father may be glorified in the Son; if you ask anything in my name, I will do it.

"If you love me, you will keep my commandments."

John 14:12–15

If the letter writer is to be believed, the Christian life is a snap, and following Jesus' charter is entirely optional. Poet Maya Angelou poignantly noted, "When somebody tells me, 'I'm a Christian,' I always say, 'Already? All these years, and *I'm still trying!*'"[4] Though joking, she was making an important point: If we are serious about following Jesus' teachings, we must never assume that we are "done" or have reached the point in life wherein we can stop holding ourselves accountable to God. Jesus never implied that human beings can reach perfection and have no need for self-examination, repentance, and redirection through prayer.

When Jesus instructed his followers, "Be perfect, therefore, as your heavenly Father is perfect," he was referring to the *life-long process* of striving to follow God's commandments and becoming increasingly attuned to God. You have been called, and pursuing this vision of what you, your child, and your family can become will require the highest commitment and determination. The best way to make sure you're on the right track is to watch yourself in action. What do you say and do that's in alignment with Jesus' teachings, and what is not? David Perkins writes, "Very often, we believe one thing, and believe we are acting accordingly, but in

> Deep in their roots,
> All flowers keep the
> light.
>
> Theodore Roethke

217

fact we act at odds with our convictions. . . . Attention to symbolic conduct can help to reveal and close such gaps."[5] In other words, to make sure we're heading in the right direction, we have to observe ourselves in action, almost as if we were strangers to ourselves; in this way, we can note how we're doing in terms of living out what we believe.

▶ **Lesson 5: To share your light, remember the place for forgiveness.** How can you share your faith in God with your child and others, whether by word or deed, if you're beating yourself up for the inevitable mistakes you'll make as a parent? Jesus taught that God seeks humble requests for forgiveness, not counterproductive and hurtful self-flagellation. He explained, after teaching his disciples the Lord's Prayer, "For if you forgive men their trespasses, your heavenly Father also will forgive you; but if you do not forgive men their trespasses, neither will your Father forgive your trespasses" (Matt. 6:14–15). This means that as long as we're willing to forgive others, we're assured that whenever we ask for forgiveness, we will receive it. Hence there's no need to get down on ourselves or to give up when we realize that we've made yet another mistake or wrong turn.

Yet it's not enough to ask God for forgiveness; we also must ask it of the person—who may be our child—whom we've failed in some way. Our culture portrays the request for forgiveness as a sign of weakness or as some kind of blanket statement that we're no good, completely awful, and a total failure. This kind of black-or-white thinking is not aligned with Jesus' thinking or his view of human beings. He saw people in all their "colors"—strong, weak, wise, foolish, mature, impulsive. We must do the same, recognizing where we've gone wrong so that we can now go right.

When you sense that something is amiss in your relationship with your child, say a prayer for strength and guidance, then arrange a one-on-one talk in a pleasant, relaxed setting. Make it clear that you really want to know what your child is feeling and what you may have done that caused anger, hurt, or discouragement. Then say *another* silent prayer, and buckle your seat belt! You must be prepared to hear things that will make you want to argue. Resist that urge. Listen instead. Try to really hear and understand what he or she is saying. If you feel sad or regretful after hearing what your child tells you, say so. Children need to know that they have an impact on us; otherwise, we seem distant and impervious, and thus they feel unimportant to us. Apologize for whatever may have led to your child's hurt feelings, and ask him or her how you can correct the problem. Work out solutions that are realistic and healing for both of you.

If it's something you can't help—such as being depressed after a divorce or a financial problem—let your child know that this situation won't go on forever and that you'll try your best to recover emotionally and be there for him or her again. It's really unfair when experts lambaste parents who are reeling from adversity for not being optimistic and upbeat around the children. Kids see right through fake cheerfulness, so it doesn't work anyway. The pressure not to let the children see the parent's feelings just makes the parent more anxious and self-critical. This doesn't help the child one bit. It's as though you're trying not to show any alarm, even though an elephant just fell through the roof. A wiser alternative is to shield your child as much as you can and let him or her know that things won't always be this difficult. Give your child hope, not deception. Hope for a better future helps children (and adults) get through painful times. And hope was Jesus' specialty: "Blessed are those who mourn, for they will be comforted" (Matt. 5:4 NIV).

> To overcome fear of failure: (1) Value your process as well as your finished product, (2) Don't make comparisons, except with yourself, and (3) Don't be lazy.
>
> Lawrence Boldt

219

▶ **Lesson 6: Allow your child to share his or her light.** Jesus taught that whoever follows him will walk more confidently, having light for the path. Jesus said, "I am the light of the world; he who follows me will not walk in darkness, but will have the light of life" (John 8:12). As our children grow, we must keep our eyes on the prize, seeking first the kingdom of God. Otherwise, we can easily lose our way when suddenly our child needs new things of us, new ways to guide or relate to them.

Jesus considered the disciples his students for a long time. They were in training. As they grew spiritually and mentally, he began giving them more and more freedom and authority. They learned, worked under him, and experienced mistakes, failures, and successes along the way. As they matured, he began to shift his role to give them more freedom and responsibilities. Then one day Jesus "promoted" them: "No longer do I call you servants, for the servant does not know what his master is doing; but I have called you friends, for all that I have heard from my Father I have made known to you" (15:15).

Shifting roles can be challenging for parents. When my older daughter began to insist that she was an adult in her early twenties, it took me quite a while to see her that way. In hindsight, the main problem was my reluctance to "promote" her. I was waiting until she was perfectly mature and wise before treating her as more of a friend than a daughter. This was made difficult because, like many parents, I didn't feel good about not seeing her as my child. I remember going through this conflict in my mind: *If I treat her as an adult, won't that be abandoning her as my child?* As a result, I went back and forth, one day treating her as a peer and the next as a little girl. She too played these two roles during that transitional period. What helped to break us out of this seesawing rut was the resolution that we made together one day: We would commit to a *series* of conversations over dinner or coffee until we both felt comfortable in our new "shoes." I had to learn how to wear the shoes of a friend, not just a mother, and she had to stop wearing only the shoes of a daughter. This then gave her greater confidence in relating with me as an equal. In a sense, I "promoted" her, letting her see that I now considered her an adult, with her own light, equal to mine, that she could now share with others.

▶

Lesson 7: For greater strength, wisdom, and support, pray daily and find other disciples to share your journey. While our private prayer, learning, and growth are essential elements of parenting as Jesus would, we magnify our influence and increase our wisdom when we share ideas, problems, questions, feelings, and friendship with one another. I have facilitated many parent groups to help families of highly sensitive, vulnerable children, and in these groups, strangers would soon become friends. Parents helped each other to problem-solve when facing difficult dilemmas, receive and give support when needed, and have some refreshing laughs together. Their lives differed in many ways, but they were alike in one important way. They all wanted to help their children overcome obstacles, grow stronger, and develop their natural talents.

Together we can do great things for our children, our families, our community, and our hurting, rudderless world. But alone, we sometimes stumble in the dark. When our light grows dim due to stress, fatigue, or overwhelming problems, we can ask for help not only from other parents (because we've *all* been there) but from God, who is on call twenty-four hours a day, seven days a week. Jesus armed his disciples with the power of prayer and promised them:

"I will not leave you desolate; I will come to you. Yet a little while, and the world will see me no more, but you will see me; because I live, you will live also. In that day you will know that I am in my Father, and you in me, and I in you. He who has my commandments and keeps them, he it is who loves me; and he who loves me will be loved by my Father, and I will love him and manifest myself to him."

John 14:18–21

"You in me, and I in you." Have any more touching words ever been spoken? Can anything compare with Jesus' fervent desire that his followers remain in his heart, and he in theirs, come what may? You are called not to a solitary task but to begin a journey toward becoming the spiritual leader that God knows you can become. You are not expected to do it alone and certainly not perfectly, but you are needed as a leader. When you consider how many lost and needy children there are in the world—including the lonely "children" inside many adults—it's clear that every one of us is needed. In fact, Jesus urged his disciples to pray for more people who care, people who will follow his teachings for the sake of all:

> When he saw the crowds, he had compassion for them, because they were harassed and helpless, like sheep without a shepherd. Then he said to his disciples, "The harvest is plentiful, but the laborers are few; pray therefore to the Lord of the harvest to send out laborers into his harvest."
>
> Matthew 9:36–38

Come together with others who may be different from you in a million ways but the same in this: They want to raise their children as Jesus would. Jesus told his disciples in his final hours on earth that he would always be with them in spirit and that the time had come for them to teach and embody all that he had taught them. "If you abide in me, and my words abide in you, ask whatever you will, and it shall be done for you. By this my Father is glorified, that you bear much fruit, and so prove to be my disciples" (John 15:7–8).

How can we bear fruit, not only for our own children and families but for our community or even the world? There are some who achieve positions of leadership; for these individuals, the potential to apply the principles that Jesus taught and exemplified is great. We need more leaders who aspire to something higher than power, prestige, or riches. Such individuals must be courageous, however, for the world doesn't value what Jesus treasured.

For the rest of us, there are many, many ways in which we can bear fruit and influence those around us. All of the examples mentioned thus far are individuals who made personal sacrifices or took risks to help a child or guide a parent. These actions were done on a small scale, but who knows what ramifications they will have one day? Who could have known that Jennie, the music student, would later make it through medical school and have a happy family of her own—because of Ms. Bartlett? Who knows how little Sean's life may have been altered for the better because his Bible school teacher, Jim, let him know that he was worthy of attention?

I've called these kinds of actions "manna parenting," because they are nourishing psychological and spiritual support and care, like food from heaven, which children receive from people other than their parents. You are not required to do manna parenting. Nobody can expect it of you. But that's what makes it so powerful and so beautiful.

Laura, a consultant who worked from home, noticed that her son Mark's six-year-old friend Nathan never seemed to want to go home. He didn't appear particularly troubled, just lonely. Even when Mark went to another friend's house, Nathan often preferred to stay with Laura, drawing quietly while she worked.

Laura went to see Nathan's parents in an effort to understand why Nathan had become clingier over the past months and discovered that they were going through a divorce. His mother said sadly that Nathan had told her it

> Education is not filling a bucket, but lighting a fire.
> William Butler Yeats

seemed more "homey" at Laura's house and that she hadn't wanted to make an issue of this during such a difficult time. Laura realized that Nathan just needed some extra support and stability, so she let him hang around whether or not Mark was in the mood to play with him. This is manna parenting. Just as Jesus spent time with strangers of all sorts, dining and talking with them, Laura spent time with a child who was feeling a bit like a stranger in his own home. She decided to shine her light for Nathan, providing him with the comfort and homeyness he needed. Eventually, as his parents settled into new routines and the discord faded away, Nathan began to spend less time at Mark's house and more time at home. Laura, in trying to follow Jesus' example, had provided a bridge for Nathan to move safely from one phase of life to the next.

Parenting is a sacred undertaking. Beneath all the tears and laughter, fun and tantrums, families provide us not only with love but with meaning. As parents, we're called to share our light with our children and others. People become heroes when they say yes to a calling that will require trying harder and staying more focused on priorities than most people ever do. There are heroes whose names are not known to the larger world but whose influence will make the difference for someone—the difference between hope and despair, between following the crowd and traveling a higher path, even between life and death. When Jesus gave that powerful man-

> I am done with great things and big things, great institutions and big success, and I am for those tiny invisible molecular moral forces that work from individual to individual, creeping through the crannies of the world like so many rootlets, or like the capillary oozing of water, yet which, if you give them time, will rend the hardest monuments of men's pride.
>
> William James

date and astounding blessing to those twelve imperfect human beings, he was calling them heroes. He said, "You are the light of the world."

Remember and Reflect

Looking back, can you remember anyone who shared his or her light with you? What kind of light was it—inspiration, faith in you, help with a problem, a needed insight, or a push to try harder?

Have you shared your light with your child or someone else? What form did it take? Did you see results right away, or did you have to content yourself with the knowledge that you had planted a seed that would grow over time?

If you could have any person, whether living now or not, share his or her light with you, who would it be? Was there someone in your family, a teacher, or someone you admired whose light you would have cherished long ago?

> **Be a light, not a judge; a model, not a critic. And have faith in the eventual outcome.**
> Stephen Covey

How do you feel—ready, afraid, needing more time or more support from

225

others—about the "call within a call" to share your light with your child, with your family, with your community, or even with the world?

With whom is Jesus asking you to share your light? In what ways would Jesus feel you need support to share your light with others?

Afterword

"Where your treasure is, there your heart will be also."
                                    Matthew 6:21 NIV

It was 8 P.M. and a raggedy old car huffed and puffed in the lane next to me. The driver, a woman in her thirties, leaned over to see whatever her young daughter was showing her. There were laundry baskets in the backseat, and the woman yawned every few moments. She looked with tired eyes of love at her daughter, dressed in a sparkly ballet costume. Had this mother been working all day, trying to make ends meet? Had she spent her last dollars on dance classes, dollars gained through long, hard hours of work? In my mind I heard strains of the old hymn "If That Isn't Love" as the light turned green and they rattled down the road. That mother's only "investment portfolio" has a ponytail and is sitting in a junky automobile, yet this child is receiving the kind of love that Jesus received from God, the kind of love that the disciples received from Jesus, and what your child receives from you.

What matters most to you? You've seen for yourself how modern society, fixated as it is on money, materialism, narcissism, aggression, and sexuality, can offer your child but fleeting pleasures, along with many weakening snares. When the inevitable problems of life arise, the inner "house" built on these values will quickly collapse. My guess is that you want much more for your child and for yourself. You want meaning, a sense of purpose, and genuine connection with your child and with others. You want to overcome obstacles within and without and to find and fulfill your calling. You want these things for your child as well. I don't need to tell you that our world is in terrible conflict, disarray, and need. Your talents and your child's talents must not be wasted. No matter what your financial, work, personal, or family situation, others need you.

It is an awesome responsibility, isn't it? Raising children seems to impact so many people, not just the child. Shouldn't we model ourselves after Jesus? Shouldn't we, as Christians, refer to Christ's teachings as we guide and make decisions about our children? Can we build a fellowship of parents who are striving to raise our children with the love, wisdom, and guidance with which Jesus would raise a child? I think we can, we should, and we will.

No army can withstand the strength of an idea whose time has come.
Victor Hugo

228

Suggested Reading

The following books have helped me as a parent as well as the families I've worked with in counseling to see, hear, guide, and talk with our children in ways that are aligned with the approach Jesus used in mentoring, shepherding, and nurturing his disciples. Caring parents and grandparents of all faiths seek to impart spiritually sound values and to strengthen their parent-child relationships. Some of these books are old reliables, and some are newer, but all have in common their practical guidance strategies and supportive parenting tips that work.

For Expectant Parents and Parents of Infants and Young Children

Dinkmeyer, Don, Gary McKay, and James Dinkmeyer. *Parenting Young Children*. Circle Pines, Minn.: American Guidance Service, 1989.

Leach, Penelope. *Your Baby and Child*. New York: Alfred A. Knopf, 1987.

Wyckoff, Jerry, and Barbara Unell. *Discipline without Shouting or Spanking*. Deephaven, Minn.: Meadowbrook Press, 1984.

For Transforming Your Family Culture, Teaching Self-Discipline, Mentoring, and Guiding Children of All Ages

Covey, Stephen. *The Seven Habits of Highly Effective Families.* New York: Golden Books, 1997.

Kaye, Kenneth. *Family Rules.* New York: Walker and Co., 1984.

For Parents Who Want to Boost Their Child's Learning and Self-Esteem

Briggs, Dorothy. *Your Child's Self-Esteem.* New York: Doubleday, 1970.

Faber, Adele, and Elaine Mazlish. *How to Talk So Kids Can Learn.* New York: Simon and Schuster, 1995.

For Parents of Teenagers and Young Adults

Dinkmeyer, Don, and Gary McKay. *Parenting Teenagers.* Circle Pines, Minn.: American Guidance Service, 1990.

Stone, Douglas, Bruce Patton, and Sheila Heen. *Difficult Conversations: How to Discuss What Matters Most.* New York: Penguin, 1999.

For the Parent Who Needs Encouragement in Times of Trouble

Goleman, Daniel. *Emotional Intelligence.* New York: Bantam, 1995.

Jones, Laurie Beth. *Jesus, CEO: Using Ancient Wisdom for Visionary Leadership.* New York: Hyperion, 1995.

Maxwell, John C. *Failing Forward.* Nashville: Thomas Nelson, 2000.

Mother Teresa and Brother Roger. *Seeking the Heart of God: Reflections on Prayer.* New York: HarperCollins, 1993.

Nelson, Alan. *Broken in the Right Place.* Nashville: Thomas Nelson, 1994.

Swindoll, Charles. *Start Where You Are.* Nashville: Word, 1999.

See Helpful Websites at: www.jesusonthefamily.org
www.attachmentparenting.org
www.parentinginjesusfootsteps.org

Notes

Introduction

1. Joseph Girzone, *A Portrait of Jesus* (New York: Doubleday, 1998), 4–5.
2. Iyer Raghavan, *The Moral and Political Writings of Mohatma Gandhi*, vol. 1 (Oxford: Clarendon Press, 1986), 518.
3. David Perkins, "Notes on Symbolic Conduct," Harvard University, December 1997.
4. Girzone, *A Portrait of Jesus*, 65.

Part 1 Our Inner Growth Comes First

1. Philip Yancey, *The Jesus I Never Knew* (Grand Rapids: Zondervan, 1995), 253.
2. Jack Mezirow, "Learning to Think Like an Adult," in Jack Mezirow, ed., *Learning as Transformation* (San Francisco: Jossey-Bass, 2000), 22.
3. Alan Nelson, *Broken in the Right Place* (Nashville: Thomas Nelson, 1994), 17–18.

Chapter 1 The Call

1. *Vine's Expository Dictionary*, "Hate," in *Bible Explorer 2.0* (San Jose, Calif.: Epiphany Software, 1999).
2. Marcus Braybrooke, *The Wisdom of Jesus* (Pleasantville, N.Y.: Reader's Digest Association, 1997), 67.
3. William Barclay, *The Gospel of Mark* in *The Daily Study Bible* (Louisville, Ky.: Westminster John Knox Press, 1975), 61–62.

Chapter 2 Servant Leadership

1. William Barclay, *The Gospel of Matthew*, vol. 1, in *The Daily Study Bible* (Louisville, Ky.: Westminster John Knox Press, 1975), 61.
2. P. Fonagy et al., "The Capacity for Understanding Mental States: The Reflective Self in Parent and Child and Its Significance for Security of Attachment," *Infant Health Journal* 13 (1991): 200–216.
3. For more on leadership in intelligent organizations, see for example David Perkins, *King Arthur's Table: How Collaborative Conversations Create Smart Organizations* (New York: Wiley, 2002).
4. Kathie Kania, "My True Colors," *Guideposts*, May 2002, 87.

Chapter 3 Jesus' Charter

1. Charles Swindoll, *Start Where You Are* (Nashville: Word, 1999), 7.
2. "In our modern English idiom the word meek is hardly one of the honourable words of life. Nowadays it carries with it an idea of spinelessness, and subservience. . . . But it so happens that the word meek—in Greek *praus* (4239)—was one of the great Greek ethical words. Aristotle has a great deal to say about the quality of meekness (*praotis* = 4236). . . . Aristotle defines meekness, *praotes* (4236), as the mean between *orgilotes* (see *orge*, 3709), which means excessive anger, and *aorgesia*, which means excessive angerlessness. . . . If we ask what the right time and the wrong time are, we may say as a general rule for life that it is never right to be angry for any insult or injury done to ourselves. . . . selfless anger can be one of the great moral dynamics of the world" (Barclay, *Gospel of Matthew*, vol. 1, 96).
3. Ibid., 89–90.
4. Edgar Schein, *Organizational Culture and Leadership* (San Francisco: Jossey-Bass, 1997).
5. Robert Kegan and Lisa Lahey, *How the Way We Talk Can Change the Way We Work* (San Francisco: Jossey-Bass, 2001).
6. Perkins, "Notes on Symbolic Conduct."

Chapter 4 Taking Care of Yourself

1. Braybrooke, *The Wisdom of Jesus*, 17.
2. Ibid.
3. Flor Hofmans, *Jesus: Who Is He?* (Belgium: Newman Press, 1966), 173–95.
4. Stephen Covey, *The Seven Habits of Highly Effective Families* (New York: Golden Books, 1997), 30.
5. Ibid.

Chapter 5 Avoiding and Resisting Temptation

1. William Barclay, *The Gospel of John*, vol. 1, in *The Daily Study Bible* (Louisville, Ky.: Westminster John Knox Press, 1975), 64.
2. Bruce Wilkerson, *The Prayer of Jabez* (Sisters, Ore.: Multnomah, 2000), 65.
3. Ibid.

Chapter 6 Spiritual Guidance

1. William Barclay, *The Gospel of Matthew*, vol. 2, in *The Daily Study Bible* (Louisville, Ky.: Westminster John Knox Press, 1975), 59.
2. Nelson, *Broken in the Right Place*, 25.

Chapter 7 Encouraging Your Child's Potential

1. See Barclay, *The Book of Luke*, 198.
2. Braybrooke, *The Wisdom of Jesus*, 61.
3. "Leaven . . . was the Jewish metaphorical expression for an evil influence. To the Jewish mind leaven was always symbolic of evil. It is fermented dough; the Jew identified fermentation with putrefaction; leaven stood for all that was rotten and bad. Leaven has the power to permeate any mass of dough into which it is inserted. Therefore leaven stood for an evil influence liable to spread through life and to corrupt it.

Now the disciples understood. They knew that Jesus was not talking about bread at all; but he was warning them against the evil influence of the teaching and the beliefs of the Pharisees and Sadducees" (Barclay, *Gospel of Matthew*, vol. 2, 131.

4. John C. Maxwell, *Failing Forward* (Nashville: Thomas Nelson, 2000), 183.

Chapter 8 Nurturing and Guiding Your Child

1. *Mother Teresa*, a film by Ann and Jeanette Petrie (1986), www.petrieproductions.com.

2. Laurie Beth Jones, *Jesus, CEO: Using Ancient Wisdom for Visionary Leadership* (New York: Hyperion, 1995), 221.

3. Douglas Stone, Bruce Patton, and Sheila Heen, *Difficult Conversations: How to Discuss What Matters Most* (New York: Penguin, 1999), 74–82.

4. Jerome Groopman, *Second Opinions* (New York: Viking Press, 2000), 9–37.

5. Jerome Groopman, "The Examined Life," *Harvard* 102, no. 5 (May–June 2000): 58–60, 103.

6. Covey, *The Seven Habits of Highly Effective Families*, 53.

7. Yancey, *The Jesus I Never Knew*, 159.

Chapter 9 Living by the Golden Rule

1. Barclay, *The Gospel of Matthew*, vol. 1, 146.

2. Girzone, *A Portrait of Jesus*, 90.

3. Aaron Beck, *Prisoners of Hate* (New York: HarperCollins, 1999), 287.

Chapter 10 Transforming Your Family to Transform the World

1. Renzo Allegri, *Teresa of the Poor* (Ann Arbor, Mich.: Charis Books, 1996), 53.

2. Barclay, *The Gospel of Matthew*, vol. 1, 122.

3. Ibid., 124.

4. Maya Angelou, *Wouldn't Take Nothing for My Journey Now* (New York: Random House, 1993), 73.

5. Perkins, "Notes on Symbolic Conduct."

Teresa Whitehurst, Ph.D., is a clinical psychologist who received her doctoral degree in clinical psychology from Vanderbilt University. She interned at the Los Angeles V.A. Medical Center specializing in neuropsychology and post-traumatic stress disorder. She did her residency at Tufts–New England Medical Center on the child psychiatry inpatient unit and consulted with families at the Boston Juvenile Court Clinic. She worked with violent teens in an inner-city clinic in Virginia and in North Carolina's program for juvenile offenders.

Dr. Whitehurst has worked with individuals and families since 1983 in a variety of settings. Her interest in "leadership parenting" grew out of her work at Harvard in the Learning Innovations Laboratories project, her experiences as a mother (she has two daughters, ages seventeen and twenty nine), and her work with families in counseling. She has recently worked on the Story Project at Harvard in the Graduate School of Education, which examined the role of dialogue in helping people from war-torn areas move from hostility and stereotyping to greater understanding and peace.

Dr. Whitehurst is a member of Christians for Nonviolent Parenting and coauthored the booklet for parents and church groups "Nonviolent Christian Parenting." She has written weekly columns in three Boston area newspapers, articles in regional magazines, and academic chapters in psychology and psychiatry texts. She is also the author of *The Practical Therapist*.

Dr. Whitehurst has appeared on weekly call-in segments of the morning show at WCMV, the NBC affiliate in Nashville, and has been interviewed and performed call-ins at various radio stations in the Boston and Nashville areas. Dr. Whitehurst has presented numerous seminars and workshops for the public.

Dr. Whitehurst can be reached through her website:
www.jesusonthefamily.org